WORDS TO LIVE BY

CHIARA LUBICH
and Christians
from all over the world

new city press, new york

Published in the United States by New City Press
the Publishing House of the Focolare Movement, Inc.
206 Skillman Avenue, Brooklyn, N.Y. 11211
© 1980 by New City Press, Brooklyn, N.Y.
Material contained in this book was translated
from *Essere la tua parola* © 1980 Città Nuova Editrice,
Rome, and *Paroles pour Vivre* © 1979 Nouvelle Cité,
Paris
Printed in the United States of America
Library of Congress Catalog Card Number: 80-82419
ISBN 0-911782-08-7

Nihil Obstat: Charles E. Diviney, P.A.
        Diocesan Censor

Imprimatur: Francis J. Mugavero, D.D.
        Bishop of Brooklyn

Brooklyn, N.Y., June 10, 1980

CONTENTS

PREFACE

"We have understood that the world needs a treatment of...the Gospel, because only the Good News can give back to the world the life it lacks. This is why we live the *Word of Life*....

"We *make it flesh* in ourselves to the point of *being* that living Word...."[1]

Here, expressed by Chiara Lubich, is the basic insight that led her and the initial members of the Focolare Movement to choose each week—and later each month—a sentence from the Gospel, to comment on it, and to live it together. This practice, which has remained constant from the beginning of the Movement is fundamental to its members' life. It does not consist in merely reflecting upon a word of the Gospel nor even in meditating upon it, but in putting it into action—in all the circumstances of daily life. It is thus lived with the conviction that the words of Jesus are "spirit and life," and that a single word of the Gospel, if it is put into practice, can be a starting point for the re-evangelization of one's whole life. Chiara Lubich uses the following image to express this

[1]All quotations in this Preface are taken from: Chiara Lubich, *The Word of Life*, New York: New City Press, 1975, pp. 43–45.

certainty: We only need to know a few letters and rules of grammar in order to read and write, but if we don't know them we remain illiterate for the rest of our lives. In the same way, a few sentences of the Gospel are enough to form Christ in us—if we live them.

Thus the Word of Life with its commentary was recopied, mimeographed, printed month after month, so that each member of the Movement, each person who wished to live it, could have it on hand, in his or her pocket, on the desk, on the night table: anywhere close by, so that it would be remembered, so that the person could be impregnated with it, and living it could become almost a reflex. Today, over a million copies of the Word of Life are distributed each month, and it is lived by people throughout the world.

Another characteristic feature of the Movement is the way its members tell each other how they live the Word of Life. Just as scientists experiment on hypotheses in laboratories and then communicate their results to one another in order to advance their science, so those who put the Word of Life into practice communicate their "experiences." This is done, not to show off virtues, but to share the light they have received.

The accounts of these experiences have certain characteristics in common: they are short stories, limited in time, showing how God reveals himself and acts; and they are an encouragement to all of us.

Thirteen Words of Life, with their commentaries by Chiara Lubich, are collected in this book. With them are a number of experiences, which have been chosen, not because of their uniqueness, but because of their ordinariness. They show that this life can be lived in all circumstances; that it unfolds in great actions as in small ones; that it can animate every person—a member of congress as much as a housekeeper. They show how this life retains its originality and power in any country, any culture. For this reason we have kept them anonymous, and have not identified their place of origin, except in special cases. Thus each reader, free of prejudice, will be able to enter into the life of the speaker and participate in the light that has been given. Some readers will be sensitive to one situation, while others will react to another. Perhaps one of these experiences will surprise or shock the reader. But no one should stop at these reactions; on the contrary, the reader should seek out what light he or she can find. The book has no other aim.

In concluding this preface, let us once again allow Chiara Lubich to speak:

"We live many words of Sacred Scripture, so that they stay with us as a permanent treasure in our souls.

"To live the Word in the present moment of our lives—this is our task.

"And all of us can live it, whatever our vocation, age, or position in society, because Jesus is Light for every human being who comes into this world.

"With this simple method we re-evangelize our souls and with them the world....

"Let us be living Gospels, living Words of Life, each of us another Jesus! Then we will really be loving him, and we will be imitating Mary, the Mother of the Light, of the Word: the living Word.

"We have no other book except the Gospel; we have no other science, no other art.

"There is Life!

"Whoever finds it does not die."

The Editor

1
The Golden Rule

"So always treat others as you would like them to treat you; that is the meaning of the law and the prophets." (Mt 7:12)

Have you ever felt a thirst for the infinite, or experienced a burning desire in your heart to live life to the fullest? Have you ever felt dissatisfied deep down inside because of what you do or what you are?

If so, you will be happy to find that there is a formula that will give you the fullness you seek, that will not leave you with regrets over days half-lived.

There is a thought-provoking sentence in the Gospel which, if understood even a little, will fill us with joy. It sums up all the laws which God has imprinted in every human heart. Here it is: *"So always treat others as you would like them to treat you; that is the meaning of the law and the prophets."*

This sentence is known as the "Golden Rule." Christ gave it to us, but it was already universally known. Not only was it contained in the Old Testament, but it was also known and taught by Seneca, Confucius and others. This demonstrates how dear it is to God's heart, and how he wants all human beings to make it the norm of their lives.

The words have a pleasant ring to them. They sound like a slogan: *"So always treat others as you would like them to treat you."*

Let's love every neighbor we meet during the day in this way, putting ourselves in their situations and treating them as we would like to be treated if we were in their place. The voice

11

of God who lives within us, will suggest the appropriate expression of love for each circumstance.

Is my neighbor hungry? Then it is I who am hungry. Let me give him something to eat.

Are others suffering injustice? Their suffering is mine. Are they experiencing darkness and doubt? Then I am, too. Let me give them words of comfort and share their pain, and not rest until they have found light and their spirits have been lifted. For that is how I would want to be treated.

Are my neighbors handicapped? Then I want to love them so much that I will be able to almost feel their handicaps in my own body and in my own heart. Love will show me what to do in order to make them feel equal to everyone else, and to help them realize that they possess an additional grace—their suffering (since we Christians know how much suffering is worth).

This is how we must behave toward everyone, without discriminating in any way between those who are pleasant or unpleasant, young or old, friends or enemies, fellow citizens or aliens, beautiful or ugly. The Gospel means everyone.

Is something within you reacting against what I've said? If so, I understand. These words of mine may seem simple, but what a change they demand! How far removed they are from our usual way of thinking and acting.

But courage! Let's try.

A day spent like this is worth a lifetime. And when evening comes, we will no longer recognize ourselves. A joy we never knew before will fill us. We will experience a new strength. God will be with us because he is with those who love. From then on, each day will be full.

At times, perhaps, we will slow down. We will be tempted to get discouraged, to stop, to go back to living as before...

But no! Take courage! God will give us the grace. Let's make a fresh start each time.

As we persevere, we will see the world around us changing. We will discover that the Gospel offers the most fascinating way of life, one that makes each day something to look forward to. We will find that the Gospel is a beacon of light in the world, that it contains the key to the resolution of all problems.

And we will not be at peace until we have communicated our extraordinary experience to others: to the friends who might understand us, to our relatives, to whomever we feel moved to share it with.

Hope will be reborn.

"So always treat others as you would like them to treat you."

Chiara Lubich

IF I WERE SICK

Every week, after reading a certain magazine, C. would give it to an old lady who lives in a nursing home. One day she slipped the Word of Life into it. The next week she went to visit the old lady and asked her if she had read the magazine. The lady replied: "The magazine, no; but the letter inside, yes!" She tapped on the table to emphasize her words: "That is life, that is something worthwhile; we must all live like this. I read it twice, and afterwards I went upstairs to visit A. who is sick. For a long time I have not had the strength to climb the stairs; but I said to myself that if I were sick, I would really want someone to come and visit me. And I was able to make it up the stairs! And I did it again! And many more times again! I read the letter to A. and we decided to live this Word together."

J.V.

THE OBTRUSIVE FRIEND

Tonight, I spent a lot of time with a friend. He had a lot of things to tell me in confidence. At a certain point, I realized that I was not a good listener: my answers were ready before he had finished speaking! Then I thought that he was possibly suffering on account of me. So I started listening intently and even sharing his suffering.

C.F.

14

THE SILLY QUESTION

Leaving Ndim in order to walk to my village, I met a man on the way who did not look like a human being. I was scared when I saw him and wanted to turn around. But right away I remembered the Gospel says: "Do not be afraid; do not fear anyone." I had the strength to pass in front of him, and he gently called me: "Uncle, uncle." I stopped. The man said to me: "I have not eaten for many days. Give me some money." I only had 200 francs for my trip. I told him I did not have anything. But the Word of Life made me change my attitude. I slipped him 100 francs right away and he thanked me warmly. Two days later I met this same man again. This time I had no money. I gave him some peanuts I had in my bag. Beside him was another fellow who asked me this silly question: "Is this many your brother?" I answered, "Yes." And he went away making fun of me.

Mark
(Ivory Coast)

TAKING THE FLOOR

One of my teachers was recovering from a serious depression which had led him to the verge of suicide. The students were not paying attention and were noisy as usual. So, before the teacher's arrival, I got up and asked to speak. I told everyone they could not continue acting this way, but had to love that man as if they were seeing him for the first and last time. The hour of class that followed was really exceptional.

P.R.

THE GOLDEN RULE

It was three o'clock in the afternoon. I was washing my hair and I was in a hurry to go out because I had a lot to do that

15

afternoon. The phone rang. When I heard the voice at the other end of the line, I panicked for a moment. It was someone who had tried to reach me often lately. He was a very unlikable person whom I had not seen in a long time and had no wish to see again. His constant aggressiveness always led me to answer with the same tone.

Anyway, for the time being, he had found me and wished to see me. I told him I had to go out and really had no time to meet him. At that point we were cut off. Maybe he had hung up but it seemed most improbable to me.

I continued to wash my hair thinking to myself: "If he is the one who hung up, that's okay; but if we were cut off, he may think that I was the one who hung up." It was true I didn't want to see him, but still—

And at that moment, I remembered: "Always treat others as you would like them to treat you." I very definitely would not want to be treated like this. He had told me that he wanted to speak with me, that he had problems. And if I had problems, would I be happy if the one I was talking to hung up because he found me unpleasant? I recalled then how I was hurt when one of my girlfriends turned her back on me some time before. Making a big effort I took the telephone directory and looked for his number. "Was it you who hung up?" I asked. "No? Then we were cut off."

The conversation picked up and the appointment was set for the next day.

During the next twenty-four hours, each time I thought of this meeting, I felt a strong revulsion. And then I thought of the Word of Life again and calm returned.

When the hour of our appointment arrived, my stomach was upset but right away I told myself: "And if I were in his shoes? When things did not go well, I was very happy to find friends."

I greeted him calmly. We had a drink together and he told me about his life during these last years: his father's death, his

16

mother's illness, the present crisis. I listened to him attentively and I saw him becoming calm, little by little.

He was surprised and happy that I did not give him any advice. I told him that he would find the real answer within himself. I realized then that I had to consider him as a mature person from now on, and not as the immature individual I once thought he was.

P.C.

"LA BALLADE DES GENS HEUREUX"

To celebrate a small event, we had promised a record to our 12 year old daughter. Since she liked Gèrard Lenorman very much, I intended to buy her "La ballade des gens heureux"— but she did not know that I had a particular record in mind. The day I was supposed to go and choose the record with her, an unforeseen circumstance obliged me to stay home, and she expressed her wish to go and choose the record alone. I was not happy, since she intended to get a different record: a very popular one that I disliked intensely.

I hesitated, and decided to love her by not expressing my personal taste and by having confidence in her. After all, I had to love her and her taste without imposing my own taste upon her.

A little later, she came back with her record: "Mother, I didn't get the record I intended to. The cover was awful. It had a heart with a half-naked woman. I took another one with a beautiful cover. I hope you don't mind." She pulled the record out of the bag. It was "La ballade des gens heureux" of Lenorman.

R.C.

UNACCEPTABLE THINGS

I gave the Word of Life to a girlfriend at work. She is our shop steward. As soon as she read the title "The Golden Rule," she made a typical unionist reflection: "If everybody acts with kindness, then we will contribute to maintaining injustice. There are some things that one should not accept."

But two weeks later, she came to ask my advice on an important matter. Then she told me that the meetings with the director and management were taking place in a much calmer atmosphere. She admitted that she read the text of the Word of Life and confided that it was very important to her even though it was not always easy.

F.T.

THE TWO CRUZEIROS

A woman had two cruzeiros. She left her house to buy food for her children's lunch. On her way to the store, she remembered a sick old lady who lived nearby. She paid her a visit and found her without either food or medicine. She looked at her two poor cruzeiros: "Always treat others as you would like them to treat you..." Putting aside her own concerns, she went out and bought the medicine for that lady and brought it back to her. Then she returned home. But to her surprise she found that her children were not there. The whole family had been invited to a birthday party at a neighbor's house.

(Brazil)

2

Love your enemies

"Love your enemies, do good to those who hate you, bless those who curse you, pray for those who treat you badly." (Lk 6:27–28)

"Love your enemies."

These are very strong words. They completely overturn our way of thinking and compel us to make a sharp turnabout in our lives.

Let's face it. We all have some enemies of one kind or another.

My enemy might be my next door neighbor or that unpleasant, meddlesome lady whom I meet in the elevator and always try to avoid.

Your enemy could be that relative who mistreated your father thirty years ago and with whom you haven't spoken since.

He could be that classmate whom you have refused to look at ever since he got you into trouble with the teacher.

She could be the girlfriend who dropped you to go out with someone else.

Or he could be the salesman who cheated you.

Sometimes we look at politicians as enemies if their opinions are different from ours.

There are people today who regard the government as their enemy and, therefore, willingly carry out acts of violence against those who represent it.

And, as always, there are people who hate the Church and, therefore, regard the clergy as their enemies.

All of these, and many, many others whom we consider enemies *must be loved.*

"Loved?"

Yes. They must be loved! However, this is not merely a matter of changing hatred into some more benevolent kind of feeling.

We have to do much more than that. This is what Jesus says: *"Love your enemies, do good to those who hate you, bless those who curse you, pray for those who treat you badly."*

As we can see, Jesus wants us to overcome evil with good. He wants us to show our love concretely.

We might wonder why Jesus is asking this of us.

The fact is he wants us to pattern our lives after the life of God, his Father, who "causes his sun to rise on bad men as well as good, and his rain to fall on honest and dishonest men alike" (Mt 5:45–46).

This is the point: we are not alone in the world. We have a Father, and we must become similar to him. Furthermore, he has the right to demand this of us because when we were still his enemies, when we were still living in darkness, he loved us first, by sending us his son who died in such a terrible way for each one of us.

"Love your enemies; do good to those who hate you."

Jerry, a young black boy from Washington, had already learned to live these words. Because of his high I.Q., he was admitted to a special class together with many white children. But intelligence alone was not enough to win him acceptance. Everyone disliked him because he was black. Then Christmas came. The other children exchanged gifts, leaving Jerry out. Naturally, the young boy cried, but when he arrived home, he remembered the words of Jesus, "Love your enemies." So, with his mother's permission, he bought gifts which he distributed with love to all of his "white brothers."

"Love your enemies...pray for those who treat you badly."

Elizabeth, a girl from Florence, was climbing the steps of a church to go to mass when, all of a sudden, a group of youngsters her own age started to make fun of her. It really hurt her. She would have liked to scream at them, but smiled instead. In church Elizabeth prayed for them. As she was leaving, they approached her and asked why she had behaved that way. She explained that she was a Christian and that, therefore, she had to love in every situation. She said this with great conviction. The following Sunday she discovered that her witness had borne fruit. When she entered the church she saw those same girls sitting attentively in the first pew.

These are examples of how children take God's word seriously. For this reason they are "grownups" in his eyes.

Perhaps we too ought to take steps to remedy certain situations in our own lives, all the more so since we will be judged by the way we judge others. We ourselves are the ones who give God the measure by which he will have to measure us. In fact, we often pray, "forgive us our trespasses *as* we forgive those who trespass against us." Therefore, let's love our enemies! Only by doing this can we heal disunity, break down barriers and build the Christian community.

Is it difficult? Painful? Does the mere thought of it keep us awake at night? Take courage. It is not the end of the world after all. It takes just a little effort on our part, and then God will do the remaining ninety-nine percent, and we will experience a boundless joy in our hearts.

Chiara Lubich

THE POLICEMAN'S CIGARETTE

I am 16 years old and I live in Paris. On election day, I accompanied my parents to the polls, and as it was very hot, I went outside to smoke a cigarette. A policeman in uniform was there. He seemed discontented. I started the conversation and offered him a cigarette. We talked about his work and I learned quite a few things. Then I told him: "You must find it strange that I talk with you. It must be very seldom that you speak with 16 year-olds." It had never happened before, he told me. I explained to him that I was trying to live according to a phrase of the Gospel each month. I told him: "You may find this ridiculous..." "Not at all," he answered. "Four or five years ago I really had faith but now it is gone. Yet my wife and son are baptized and go to church regularly." Then a friend of mine arrived as well as some of the policeman's colleagues, wearing civilian clothes; we were a group of five or six, pleasantly talking with one another.

At the end everybody left. The policeman took a pack of cigarettes out of his pocket and offered me one. I thanked him. I thought this was terrific. I did not think that a policeman would be so open. Since the polls were closing, he shook hands with me. Leaving he said, "So long, I hope we'll see each other again."

J.C.

A woman who used to attend daily mass received a telegram from her brother announcing the tragic death of his wife and asking her to come. But she had never been on good terms with her sister-in-law, who had prevented her brother from coming when their mother was dying. Her friends, all of them "good Christians," were setting her against her brother, telling her that she was right not to go and see him, since he himself had not come to see their mother. As a Christian she prayed for her sister-in-law, but still she did not want to go.

We who were living the Word of Life knew her well. Each month she had been taking a copy of the commentary on the Word of Life, and she kept them all because she said they were beautiful. That evening we spoke a little with her and gave her the Word of Life, "Love your enemies." Not long afterward, she came back to see us. She had a radiant face and announced that she had finally gone to see her brother and that she was reconciled with him.

Y.T.

WASN'T JESUS A JEW?

Recently, I met a young Muslim in the university cafeteria. He is training here as a work inspector, and will return to his country when he finishes his studies. We had a very simple and beautiful conversation, and I gave him the commentary on the Word of Life, "Love your enemies," asking him to let me know what he thought of it next time we met.

When I met him again he told me that he liked the text very much, and that similar things were written in the Koran. Another time he told me that for him there was a difficult aspect to living this Word—the relationship between Muslims and Jews. And he gave me examples, saying that even here in X. if he happened to ask for directions or information from a

Jew on the street the Jew would not answer. He reminded me above all of what was happening in the Middle East, and said how much he disagreed with their way of doing things.

I listened, simply trying to show him that the wrong does not come from one side only, and gave some examples of little situations where love alone had changed things. He had already told me that he esteemed Christians. At a certain point he asked me: "But Jesus was a Jew, wasn't he?" That was my chance to tell him everything which seemed positive to me in the character of the Jews, their customs and their sense of the family. The young man then told me that he would try to love the Jews as well and would go beyond his initial reactions from now on.

G.C.

THE SMALL CAR

Anyone who knows Paris is aware that having a car there is no longer a luxury, and is sometimes a necessity. We have a car, but we have friends who don't. And some of them are only too aware that we have committed ourselves to living the Gospel and that, therefore, we are willing to share what we have—including the car.

It so happened that a friend who wished to visit an amusement park with other friends, asked to borrow our old Renault. Everything was arranged. But our friend altered his plans, and did not return the car as he had promised.

The next day—a very busy one—many things had to be done by car, but we had no means of transportation. Since I had an appointment, I was beginning to get nervous and frustrated. I telephoned to find out what had happened to our car, and was assured that my friend had driven it to the swimming pool and would certainly return it soon. I started to consider using public transportation even if it meant a much longer trip, but decided to wait instead, since it would be a very quick trip once I had the car.

Time passed, but the car did not appear. Within me the tension mounted. I could see my "enemy's" face taking shape in front of me. All kinds of insults kept coming to my mind. At the same time, however, a little something—I do not know what—was pushing through my turbulent thoughts, reminding me of the Word of Life, and little by little it pacified me. Then came a phone call from my "enemy." I surprised myself saying: "Well, did you have a good swim?" Since my friend had expected to be bawled out he was quite surprised, and later, when he returned the car, he thanked me profusely.

Paul

SOLIDARITY

Saturday evening. It had been dark for some time. The mass had ended and it was nearly eight o'clock. I came out last, as usual. I had left my bicycle to the left of the door. Automatically, I reached for the key of the lock and looked for the bike... Nothing. It was gone.

Without a bike, how could I possibly be at work at seven o'clock each morning? Where would I get money to buy another? Would I have to go by bus, which would take three times longer?

I ran back into the church and grabbed the first person I met, a complete stranger, and exclaimed: "They have stolen my bike!" I do not know what he answered, but he sort of took over, and, quite helpless, I followed him. His name was James. I had to tell my story to two or three more people who had various reactions. Among others, the pastor and someone called Patrick implored me not to have someone jailed for a "piece of scrap." Finally I went home. I had a hard time falling asleep that night: a battle raged within me between the desire

27

for revenge and the lesson I had learned—"One must love even his enemies."

But the Lord passed by that night. First my landlady, feeling sorry for me, loaned me money and directed me to a flea market where, on Sunday morning, I might possibly find an old bike for sale. Once there, I found only one bike that could fit my needs, but at a very reasonable price.

When I returned I found a note from James asking me to go to the rectory. To my great surprise I learned that the community, alerted by the pastor of the parish, had gotten together and collected more than half the price of the bicycle I bought at the flea market.

I realized that a chain of solidarity had been forged by James, the pastor, my landlady and the parish community. For my part, despair was gone and forgiveness replaced revenge. I had also learned two lessons: God starts working when I stop being agitated; and he fills me with his goods when I accept the loss of mine.

J.P.

EVEN AMONG FRIENDS

I spent a two-day meeting with some friends. I could not imagine I had enemies among the people with whom I live in community and share a deep evangelical life. Yet the stories of two of them, Chris and Joe, left me confused. Deep inside of me, I did not agree with what they were saying: both have strong personalities and were expressing their choices, but I could not find the love in their way of living.

I was perhaps the only one to feel like this and I was not sure that I was right. Later, during the same meeting, I was a little aggressive towards Joe. It was a deliberately chosen aggressiveness, even marked with a certain wickedness. To make matters worse, Chris and Joe were given a delicate mission to perform as the representatives of the group.

"Accustomed" to love, I made an effort to believe that this was all right and I had even approved this choice, but deep inside a whole part of myself refused it. The next Sunday, during mass, the Word of Life came to my mind as a light: "Love your enemies." It was true: I had had hostile feelings, I had harbored misgivings without expressing them and all this was not Gospel.

I had to do quite a rapid repair job; but in the afternoon of the same day, I felt that I had changed my attitude, and meeting Joe, I felt free. The deep friendship uniting us had recovered all its fullness.

P.L.

ENEMIES BECAUSE OF A LADDER

The scarcity of ladders in the store always provokes disputes between the salespeople, and it is a real problem because each department requires one permanently. I work in the record and book department and I am practically the only one who does not need one. One morning, the saleslady from "House-wares" asked me to keep close watch over the ladder she had finally found because she had to go away for a minute and would use it later. I assured her that I would keep it. But Helen, who is in charge of "Kitchen Appliances," came along and grabbed the ladder.

"If you do not mind, Helen, Mrs. X asked me to keep it for her a few minutes."

"Open your eyes! Her name is not written on it!"

This answer seemed unkind to me and I received it as a slap in the face. I was put out. The ladder was gone, and furthermore, for the first time, I had a very tense relationship with Helen who was held in poor esteem by the others. This lasted a long time, and I was always ill at ease. Whenever we passed one another, she would not speak or greet me. On the other hand I could not make myself go toward her.

Wanting to live this Word, "Love your enemies," I felt that I had to make peace. One afternoon, not thinking of anything in particular, I went to get a drink from the soft drink machine. Helen was there all by herself. I understood that God had placed her there at that instant. I started speaking and smiled at her, trying to establish a true relationship, and with joy I saw her relaxing. Ever since, everything has been fine between us.

R.B.

BABBLING DURING MASS

One Sunday, at mass, three teenage boys—one of whom used to take up the collection—were sitting side by side in the front pew and were babbling so openly that they were distracting everybody.

I, the celebrant, was boiling with interior anger as I stood behind the altar. During the homily I felt like calling attention to them, but right away I recalled the Word of Life: "Love your enemies." I therefore had to love them and leave them babbling. Jesus was not asking me to establish order but simply to love.

After a while they fell silent and two of them, spontaneously, got up after the homily to take up the collection.

D.G.

WORDS THAT "DO SOMETHING"

I have a neighbor with a loud voice and colorful vocabulary, who does not mince words when she is annoyed. But the other day, coming back from the market, I found her very calmly explaining to a boy who lived in our building what he should and should not do on the stairs. I was amazed at her peace, because normally she would have been shouting.

A few days later, this same neighbor entered my kitchen and her eyes fell on the Word of Life on the wall. "For sure," she said, "these 'Words' do something! The other day for example, I could no longer get mad at that boy! It was stronger than I!"

C.L.

GRANDPA'S OVERCOAT

I was typing the commentary on the Word of Life, "Love your enemies." Suddenly I was struck by the words, "Your enemy could be that relative who mistreated your father...." I stopped typing. Those words were meant for me. I recalled that since my father's death, I had not wanted to see my grandfather, because he was a friend of the man who killed my father, and because he had sold some family land that my brothers should have received.

I remembered also that not long ago my mother had told me that my grandfather needed an overcoat, but I was so angry that I didn't even answer her. Later, during summer vacation, my brother told me the same thing. I replied, "I have no money to waste on someone who sold our land!" Then I asked what he thought about it, and he said that if he himself had the money, he would buy it for him. I snapped back: "You can both go to hell!"

My father died fours years ago, but after that phrase from the Word of Life it seemed as if it had all happened yesterday. For three days and nights I could think of nothing else. It was as though Jesus himself was telling me: "You did not recognize me in this man." Finally, I bought a coat and a pair of trousers and sent them to him.

I am happy now because I was able to forgive and forget.

S.F.
(Kenya)

31

My enemy Freddie

Among my usual "enemies" there are my children. I would like to see them in bed early enough to make my evenings at home a little freer, especially since some evenings I must go out. It is always a difficult process, and bedtime seldom comes before 9:30 or even 10:00 p.m.

I was reflecting on this Word of Life the other night, while my "enemy" Freddie was amputating a good portion of my evening. Overcoming my own feelings, I spent a little longer talking with him and took time to say evening prayers with him, relating our prayer to his day and his evening.

C.B.

A different sort of trip

I work in a bank and I have been a trade unionist for a good many years. It is not easy because, even without wanting to, one makes enemies. It often happens that people who disagree with the union leadership resent me. And since I am not the type to take it, I retort with all the arguments in my possession.

Once I had to go to a town to speak with people who did not approve of the line followed by the union. I knew how everything would turn out and I would have liked to find some good excuses not to go. But I felt that I could not act like that: that to love meant going there in order to listen to these people as much as I could. The Word of Life was decisive. All these people were really enemies. But contrary to my usual tactics I did not go at them with statistics and well-sharpened arguments. I was there with the will to listen and, at the end, to my great surprise, I realized that all was going well. And furthermore—something extraordinary—we all agreed, without anybody thinking that he or she had lost face.

F.N.

F., one of my co-workers, is of the Bahai religion, which, she explained, tries to be the synthesis of all the others. In order to live peacefully together at work, each one of us in harmony with our respective faiths, we made a pact: to always be "open" to the others. For this reason she listened attentively to me one day, when I told her about the "Word" we were living that month: "Love your enemies." For her it was a completely new idea, nearly illogical; and besides, upon reflection, it seemed to her that if, indeed, she had any enemies, they deserved to be treated badly.

"I take my revenge in loving them twice as much!" The answer had escaped me, and too late I realized how provoking it might be to her. I held it responsible for the silence that fell between us following this brief exchange. But the following day she came up to me: "I have been thinking over what you said. It will take me at least a month to be able to do it!"

We did not speak about it again, but when we meet, I can see she is happier than before. And a new joy marks our relationship because of this new commitment undertaken together.

M.H.

At school our French teacher got very angry at the whole class one day. Among other things, she said that she would no longer permit anyone to express his or her personal ideas nor let anyone complain to her about his or her difficulty in French. During lunch, two of my classmates decided to counterattack by writing slogans on the walls asking that she be fired. I could not agree with this approach, but I did not really know what to do.

I asked God's help and went to speak with these two classmates who were already inciting the whole class against the teacher. I tried to tell them that maybe it was not the best way to make our teacher understand that she had done a stupid thing and that it might be better to go and talk to her about it.

During the next class the two protesters were sitting behind me. One of them asked me for my physics book which I lent him right away. But then I realized that I had left the Word of Life in it: "Love your enemies" and, turning back, I saw that they were reading it. They asked me: "What's this?"

I asked the Holy Spirit to lend me a hand.

A little later, after explaining what it was all about, I proposed to them to put it into practice right away toward this teacher. They agreed!

The next morning, after discussing it among ourselves, we went to find our "enemy" to explain our point of view while trying to love her. She said that she had been wrong, that she wanted to apologize, and she added: "Above all, thank you for the way in which you have spoken to me."

And now she also is trying to live the Word of Life.

S.K.

3

An inexhaustible gift

"Give, and it will be given to you. A good measure, pressed down, shaken together and running over, will be poured into your lap." (Lk 6:38)

Has it ever happened that you received a gift from a friend and then felt you had to reciprocate—not so much because you felt obliged to pay the person back, but simply out of love and gratitude? I'm sure it has.

If you feel this way, imagine how God must feel, God who is love.

He reciprocates every gift that we give to any neighbor in his name. True Christians experience this frequently. And each time it is a surprise. We can never get used to God's imaginative tactics.

I could give you a thousand examples of this; I could even write a book about it. And you would see how true are the words: *"A good measure, pressed down, shaken together and running over, will be poured into your lap."* God always reciprocates with generosity. Here is an example.

Night had fallen in Rome. In their basement apartment, a small group of young women who wanted to live the Gospel were just wishing one another good night, when the doorbell rang. Who could it be at that hour? At the door they found a panic-stricken young father. He was desperate: the following day he and his family were going to be evicted because they hadn't paid their rent.

The women looked at one another and then, in silent accord, went to the dresser drawer. There they kept what was left of their salaries and in envelopes marked "gas," "electricity," and "telephone," the small deposits they had set aside toward these bills. Without a moment's worry about what would happen to them, they gave all the money to their visitor.

That night they went to bed very happy. They knew Someone else would take care of them.

But just before dawn the phone rang. It was the same man. "I've called a taxi and I'm coming right over!" Amazed that he should have chosen to come by taxi, they awaited his arrival. As soon as they saw his face they knew something had changed. "Last night, as soon as I got home, I found I had received an inheritance I never dreamed I would get. My heart told me I should give half of it to you." The amount he gave them was exactly twice the sum they had generously given him.

"Give, and it will be given to you. A good measure, pressed down, shaken together and running over, will be poured into your lap."

Haven't you also experienced this? If not, remember that the gift must be given with no self-interest, without hoping to get it back, and to whomever asks.

Try it. But not so that you can see if it works, but because you love God.

You might be tempted to say: "I have nothing to give." But that's not true. If we want to, each of us will find that we possess endless treasures: our free time, our love, our smile, our advice, our peace, our words that might persuade someone who has, to give to someone who has not...

You might also say: "I don't know whom to give to." Well, just look around you: don't you remember that sick person in the hospital, that widow who is always lonely, that boy in your class who failed and is so discouraged, that young man who is sad because he can't find a job, your little sister or brother who needs a helping hand, that friend who's in prison, that new person on the job who's so unsure of herself. In each of these Christ is waiting for you.

Put on the new way of behavior that comes from the Gospel and is the mark of a Christian. It is just the opposite of close-mindedness and concern for self. Stop putting your trust in this world's goods and start relying on God. This will show your faith in him, and you will soon see from the gifts that you receive that your faith is well-founded.

It is evident, however, that God does not give as he does in order to make us rich. He acts in this way so that many, many others, seeing the little miracles that happen to us as a result of our giving, may decide to do the same.

God also gives to us because the more we have the more we can give. He wants us to be administrators of his goods and to see to it that they are distributed throughout the community around us, so that others might be able to say as they said of the first Christian community: "There were no needy among them" (Acts 4:34).

Don't you think that in this way you too can help to give a solid spiritual basis to the social change that the world is waiting for?

"Give, and it will be given to you."

When Jesus said these words, undoubtedly he was thinking first and foremost of the reward we will receive in heaven. But the reward we receive on this earth is already a foretaste and a guarantee of our heavenly reward.

Chiara Lubich

THE PARKING METER

The train station seemed to welcome me that evening, since I was able to find a parking space without difficulty. I opened the door and as I got out, a begging hand was extended toward me: "Fifty cents for the subway?"

How was I to answer this neighbor quickly since my train was approaching? I reached for some change and found only two coins—exactly what I needed for the parking meter. I did not have time to go for change and I was about to say "No!" when a sentence I had read during those days crossed my mind: "Give and it will be given to you." It was a sentence that Jesus had said, and therefore a sentence to live. Without hesitation then, I gave him the two coins. As I locked the door of the car, the possibility of getting a ticket began troubling me. But I rejected the idea, holding onto my first impulse, the one that pointed beyond the limits of my reasonable heart. Then I looked at the meter that was bound to penalize my deed. Surprise! There was an hour and a half of parking already paid—three times as much as I needed.

But it was more than a surprise: it was a special joy which filled me and made me say "Thank you!"

P.P.

THE MELODY RETURNS

Lately, getting up in the morning, there has been a melody in my soul. Not this morning. After ringing the bell for mass, I went and gave the cement bags to Gregory and the others so they could make the repairs on the wells. Gregory carried the first bag to the door by himself; I let him do it because "I am going to say mass and do not want to dirty my hands..." Then for the second and third bags I helped him...and the melody returned.... Yes, God gives, and in abundance.

Léon
(Africa)

THANK YOU

A letter from Japan to Chiara Lubich: "I want to thank you on behalf of the people of the Far East: at last, with your commentary, the Word of Life has become understandable and applicable even in the lives of non-believers or of believers of other religions."

JESUS WILL NOT LET HIMSELF BE OUTDONE

Sunday evening, on the way home, it started raining. At that moment I saw a young man asking for a lift. I picked him up and told him that I was going as far as F. He was going 7 km further. As we talked I discovered it was the fourth time that day he had done the return trip, since his parents had just moved. It then started raining hard. Without saying a word I continued on past F. "Didn't you say you were stopping here?" "Yes, but the way it's pouring down, I know *I* would prefer not to be left in the rain!" My passenger was surprised and pleased.

At that moment I was not expecting anything in return, but I know that Jesus never lets himself be outdone.

41

Monday evening I got into the car and noticed a piece of paper on my windshield. I looked at it: "I bumped your car while parking, here is my telephone number...." Inspecting the car, I saw that the right fender had been dented, as well as the front door.

Soon the car will be back in good shape again!

F.M.

THE RECORD

Nearly everyone agreed it was a wonderful weekend. More than a hundred of us were reunited again—from Lyon, Toulouse, Nice, and other places. Nevertheless, I did not fully share the joy of my friends because I was rather tired and had a lot of things on my mind. Besides not sharing their joy, I had given only half smiles to those around me. When it came time for the return trip Sunday afternoon, I was asked to give my seat in the car to someone else and to travel in a small van which had not yet been broken in. It was a three hundred and fifty kilometer trip. I wouldn't be home before midnight! I felt angry at everyone, and during the trip I surely was not loving.

Halfway home, we had to stop so that someone could change places with the driver because the glare from the sun had given him a headache. Norman made a suggestion: "My parents live nearby. We could stop there for supper, and afterward you would feel better." Rotten luck! We would lose another hour. After some hesitation the van took the direction of his home. We got out. A warm welcome: his parents were so happy to see their son again and to receive us. In a jiffy the table was set, although there were seven of us.

I tried to take part in the general conversation, pretending a good humor I was far from having. Scenes from my day flashed before my eyes: a lot of negative. Not all, however: I had bought a record that morning (after having tried to do so twice)—it was meant to be given away at the first opportunity, since I did not have a record player. What if I went out to the van and got it? Norman was very pleased with the idea. It was Father's Day besides!

We left. Now there was no longer a sour note. Someone told me: "I was asking myself what could we ever offer them so as to thank them for their warm welcome."

Another one added: "You could see how happy they were! You had an *excellent idea.*" And since I smiled, he added, "Are you laughing at me?"

"No." But if he knew why I found my smile again—the trip in the van...the headache...so many occasions must have been given me.... Time seemed to have stopped and our driver, who no longer had a headache, began to speak to us of things that can only be spoken of when there is full harmony among us.

J.V.

THEY HAVE NO MILLET

My farm is far from the city, near a little village. One of my neighbors there had had a death in the family and, as is customary, many visitors had come to spend a three-day mourning period at his house. However, he did not have enough food to feed them. I had managed to get some millet, a sack nearly full. So I said to my wife: "Woman, they have no millet. Could we not share ours with them?" My wife agreed and gave some millet to this neighbor.

A few days later, I was in the field and along came the neighbor with his plow and oxen. He offered to plow my field. I told him: "No, thank you, I have no money to pay you."

But he answered me: "You were very good to us. I am happy to plow your field for free."

The plowing of the field would have cost 3,000 francs. I

thought to myself: "Jesus' words are true: Give and God will give to you."

Albert
(Chad)

I live in a small village. The other day I was at home preparing the meal. I was thinking of preparing cabbage soup but had only a little cabbage. After I had washed and cut it, a neighbor came to ask me if I had any cabbage. I gave her everything I had.

The same evening another neighbor offered me some cabbage. It amounted to three times more than what I had given.

Another time I was all by myself at home and a child of a very poor family came to play in the house. He fell down with a glass in his hand and cut himself badly. We only had 300 escudos at home. I went to the doctor with the child and this cost me 295 escudos. Therefore, my mother and I had only 5 escudos left to live on till the end of the month.

Nevertheless, with faith in God, I went to school with peace in my heart. In the evening when I returned home, one of my brothers had brought home 2,000 escudos, my mother had found 150 which she thought she had lost, and the mother of the wounded child, with barely enough money to feed her family, had found 500 escudos and came to reimburse the medical expenses.

Another time I had a craving for candy but had none at home. I wanted to buy some but did not do it because I had decided not to act as a "bourgeois" person, and to give all I had to God. The same evening a girl friend gave me a gift of a box of candies. I offered some to my girl friends, I ate one and I wanted to give the rest to my mother. But to act like this seemed to me to be false, because I really wanted to share all I

44

had. So I gave the candies to a lady in the village for her children.

When I returned home, I found two small bags of candies a girl friend had given my mother.

A.G.
(Portugal)

SIMONE

A few days before Easter, we were told about a young girl in the hospital who had just given birth and needed at least moral support.

At first my husband and I wavered. Then, trusting in God's love, we decided to go to the hospital, telling ourselves that God himself would give her what we could not.

Simone was very surprised to see two strangers coming to visit her, but a relationship was soon established.

Bit by bit we learned of her story: She came from a poor family and had moved to the city while very young to serve as a maid so as to help her parents. For the past three years she had been engaged to a boy who left her as soon as he learned she was pregnant. In spite of all the advice of her girl friends who were pressing her to have an abortion, and even in spite of the offer of a substantial sum from her boyfriend to pay for an abortion, she had brought her pregnancy to term. Now, she was going to stay in a home for unwed mothers for a while.

Whenever we had a moment, we went to see her. Once she told us about her financial troubles. For many years she had supported her family; it was the first time she ever asked for something. My husband and I decided on the spot to give her the amount she needed.

The very same day we received an unexpected check for $100.00 as a belated wedding present from a distant relative. This clearly showed us the imagination of Providence and the truth of the Gospel which says: "Give and it will be given to you."

But we were also looking for some suitable work for Simone who would soon have to leave the home. So without respite we kept asking our heavenly Father to find a job for her.

We felt the need to share our concern with a group of families we know. And it was wonderful to see the real communion of goods that took place, something that far surpassed the amount we had given at first. We saw clearly in this the "good measure, pressed down, shaken together and running over" that the Gospel speaks about. Because of this same "communion," Simone found a job: a family took her on as a housekeeper, allowing her to work and keep her child with her.

R.P.

4

Renounce yourself

"If anyone wants to be a follower of mine, let him renounce himself and take up his cross every day and follow me." (Lk 9:23)

Don't think that just because you are in the world you can take to it like a fish to water.

Don't think that simply because the world comes into your home through certain radio and television shows, you are entitled to listen to every broadcast and watch every program.

Don't think that just because you walk through the streets of the world you can look at all the ads and billboards with impunity and buy just any publications from the newsstand or the bookstore.

Don't think that just because you are in the world you can live as you please, the way the world does, and follow the world's example of immorality, abortion, divorce, hatred, violence, theft....

No! No! You are in the world; no one can deny that. But you are not *of* the world.

This fact makes a great difference. It places you among those who don't live according to what the world says, but rather according to what the voice of God suggests to you from within. God lives in the heart of every human being. If you listen to him he will lead you into a kingdom which is not of this world, a society in which true love, justice, purity, meekness and evangelical poverty are lived, where self-control is the norm.

In recent years many young people have journeyed to India and the Far East, hoping to find some peace of mind and to discover the secrets of the Eastern spiritual masters, who, after a long process of self-mortification, frequently radiate a more genuine kind of love that touches everyone who meets them.

The quest of these young people is a very natural reaction to the uproar in the world, to the noise around us and within us which leaves no room for silence in which to hear God's voice.

But is it really necessary to go to India, when for two thousand years Christ has been saying to us: *"Renounce yourself...renounce yourself"?*

A Christian cannot expect to lead a comfortable and easy life. Christ did not, and he will not ask any less of you if you want to follow him.

The world is coming at you head-on, like a river in flood, and you must go against the current. The world is like a dense underbrush in which the Christian must look very carefully where to step. And where *should* you step? In the footsteps which Christ himself laid down for you while he was passing through this world; these footsteps are his words. Today he is telling you once more: *"If anyone wants to be a follower of mine, let him renounce himself...."*

If you follow Christ, you may be laughed at, misunderstood, scorned, slandered, isolated. You must be ready to lose face, to give up the easygoing, socially acceptable way of being a Christian.

And that's not all: *"If anyone wants to be a follower of mine, let him renounce himself and take up his cross every day and follow me."*

Whether you like it or not, suffering is a part of everyone's life, yours as well. Sufferings great and small come our way every day.

Do you try to avoid them? Do you rebel against them? Do you feel like cursing them? Then you are not a Christian.

A Christian loves the cross; he or she loves each suffering, even amidst tears, knowing that suffering has a value. God had innumerable ways at his disposal by which he could have saved humankind. When he chose to use suffering, he did it for a reason.

But remember—after he had carried the cross and been crucified, Jesus rose.

Resurrection is also your destiny if, instead of despising the sufferings that come with living a consistant Christian life, and the other sufferings that each day brings with it, you accept them with love. By doing so you will see that even here on earth the cross is a way that leads to a joy you have never before experienced. You will begin to grow spiritually, and the kingdom of God will become firmly established in you. Little by little the world around you will fade away before your eyes, and will seem to be made of cardboard. And you will no longer envy anyone.

Then you will be able to call yourself a follower of Christ: *"If anyone wants to be a follower of mine, let him renounce himself and take up his cross every day and follow me."*

And like Christ whom you have followed, you will be light and love for the countless suffering people in today's world.

Chiara Lubich

A SURPRISE IN THE MAIL

For the past few weeks I have been helping a person in my neighborhood who is having a lot of family difficulties, and each step of the way I have tried to share the weight of her burden with my presence.

But today, a cunning desire for rest is tempting me; it has cleverly disguised itself with beautiful pretenses inviting me to stop for a while. After all, I deserve it, don't I? So here I am, without the least scruple, settling down quietly to open my mail.

Well! A different envelope? A text?

The Word of Life for this coming month...

Yes, this "Word" arrived just in time, when my love was getting tired!

C.P.

TOUCHING THE GOODNESS OF GOD

Relations have always been very difficult with my family, especially with my mother—to such an extent than nobody even came to visit me when I had an operation for appendicitis not long ago. After living the Word of Life for many months, I told myself that I was the one who had to take the first step.

One morning my mother phoned to tell me that my father had sold his business and was going to give all the money to my brother. It was a blow to me but, in order to avoid a conflict with her, I did not say anything. When I put down the receiver I was very upset.

Their rejection hurt me, especially coming, as it did, at a moment when I did not have much money and had been wondering for some time how I was going to buy the clothes my children needed.

The more I thought about it the more upset I became, until, at a certain moment, I understood that only the word of God could help me. I took the sheet of the Word of Life and went into the kitchen to read it.

As soon as I sat down, I was taken by the title "Renounce yourself." Immediately a great peace came over me, and I felt a joy I had never experienced before.

Afterward, I had the impression of touching the goodness of God with my finger because, in the afternoon, when I went to pick up the mail I found in it a letter with a check for $225.00. It was the reimbursement of a loan I made to a friend so long ago that I was no longer counting on it. It was just the money I needed to buy the clothing for my children. My joy at that point was boundless and I understood why we tell one another our "experiences." We are actually telling what God is doing in our lives.

M.G.

VACATION TIME

It was July, and my colleague at work was on vacation. One day, I received a call for her: she was being offered the opportunity to transfer to another city where for the past year she had been hoping to go and live. The position had to be filled by the first of August.

It was great for her, but what about me? I was due to take my vacation from the 1st to the 24th of August. Yet we were the only two who could do the work; and it was impossible to close the office. It seemed that either my colleague would leave and I would lose my vacation, or I would leave and my colleague would lose the job for which she had waited so long. How could such a situation be reconciled with the Word of Life?

I tried to have confidence in God. I did not get upset, I did not ask to see the director; I resigned myself to giving up my vacation so as to let her go. Upon her return on the 18th of July, my colleague explained to me that she had to begin her new job on the 16th of August, at the latest.

I have to admit that this Word of Life was no longer very easy to live. I advised her to fix a meeting for us with the management; but I was quite distressed. In the meantime I happened to speak with a friend who turned the question around, pointing out that by "renouncing" "my" vacation, I was also sacrificing my family's. They had been waiting for this vacation for a long time, since we have not had one in the past few years.

The end of the day brought a great gift: my colleague would not be leaving until my vacation was over, and the management would see to it that the new position would be held for her, even after the fixed date.

B.S.

FATHER'S DAY GIFT

Like everyone else, I undergo the daily aggressions that advertising, fashion, etc. wage against us. All this causes the spirit to deviate from the search for God. So many precious moments are wasted daydreaming while gazing at a poster or an attractive person; so many instants lived negatively, only for ourselves. I understood this last year during a meeting of the Movement. Indeed, meeting Jesus in many people who were living the Word showed me that if I wanted to continue to look for this kind of relationship with each person I met in my everyday life, I had to be able to master my gaze, and love, each person as Jesus in him or her wants me to.

At that time I was given the precious advice of not trying to fight the difficulty head-on. If I could not find the way out of it by myself, it was better to share it with others in order to overcome it more easily. From time to time I kept entrusting this difficulty to the Lord and to Mary, but I did not have enough faith, I was too timid in asking, for fear that I would fall again. And I did fall.

It was also very evident to me that we couples should desire this purity. Each partner is there, not to fulfill a supposed personal need, but—on the contrary—to learn how to give. Give; in other words: no thought for self.

So this month, thanks to this Word of Life, I had the strength to give to God that part of myself I had been keeping with the excuse that I was weak. I had to give him everything, without trying to know whether I could keep from failing. To give him everything because that is what he asks in exchange for his grace.

In order to take this step, I wanted to prepare myself a little: I cannot take part in the Eucharist every day, but on this occasion it seemed to me important to make an effort to do so. I must say that I received quite a smack in the face that day! The Gospel of the day was Mt 5:27–32, "Anyone who looks at a woman lustfully has already committed adultery with her in his heart. If your right eye causes you to sin, gouge it out...." and the rest!

I was anxiously awaiting the comment of the priest to learn how to "gouge out my right eye." Silence! Nothing! Then I understood in all its strictness the love of God for me and that I had to respond to this love right away. It was the gift that I owed him...for Father's Day.

G.M.

Having suffered a dreadful blow in my relationship with the town hall, where I work as a librarian, I had spoken of my situation in a group of the I.C.A. (Independent Catholic Action) where we studied it. In fact the theme for reflection for this year is "to live it together."

Since the beginning of May, I have tried to live the Word of Life. It is really difficult to love the mayor of my small town, who has deceived me and slandered me in public. Unable to do it so far, I am satisfied in not preventing the townspeople from loving him. In telling them all that has happened (as I am obliged to do, since they have the right to the information) I try to do it without hate and without excuses (there are some).

Yesterday we had a meeting in order to share all the work of the members of the diocesan I.C.A. Quite unexpectedly, our bishop was present. He worked with us, read the reports of all the teams and at the end of the meeting, he made a spiritual synthesis of them all and then said: "The case of the library merits our special attention because it represents a great suffering caused by a gross injustice, but you must tell the librarian (he did not know who I was or that I was present) that Jesus trusted the greatest sinners: Pilate, Peter, Mary of Magdala and all the others, even his worst enemies. If this librarian wants to live for Jesus, she must also restore her trust. Let her know also that in order to go ahead, one must die to oneself, but that is possible only with the help of the Spirit of Jesus. May she find peace again; the work she has done is not lost. As a servant of God, she has opened the road to love, the only road to fruitfulness."

I was the one in charge of writing down the minutes of the meeting, and it was quite hard to write under the dictation of Jesus himself who came to give me again the meaning of my work and suffering through the mouth of our bishop.

The members of my I.C.A. group who know how I try to live the Word understood, I think, what I felt and were astonished by it. One of them said to me: "You have been comforted and visited by Jesus himself this evening. All of us have been witnesses and beneficiaries of it."

C.L.

YOU WILL BE LIGHT AND LOVE

I gave the Word of Life to a woman who works in the fields. She put down the vegetables she was carrying and asked me to read it to her. It ends with the words "you will be light and love for the countless suffering people in today's world." When I had read these words, the woman, who had been listening with her head in her hands, looked up at me and said: "Now I have the strength to make the decision: I'm going to go to the bar and get my husband and tell him that I want to live with him again."

M.B.

5

The right choice

"Not my will but yours be done." (Lk 22:42)

Do you recall these words? They are the words Jesus addressed to the Father in the Garden of Gethsemane, and they give meaning to his passion and death, followed by his resurrection. They reveal, in all its intensity, the drama taking place within Jesus, the inner agony brought on by the utter revulsion his human nature felt in the face of the death willed by the Father.

Christ, however, did not wait until that day in order to conform his will to God's will. He had been doing it all his life.

If this is how Christ lived, then his attitude must also be the attitude of every Christian. You too must repeat with your life: *"Not my will but yours be done."*

Perhaps you never thought of this before, even if you are baptized and a churchgoer.

Perhaps you have reduced these words to a mere expression of resignation—something you say when you have no choice. This, however, is not the correct interpretation.

Listen. In life you can go in one of two directions: you can do your own will, or you can freely choose to do God's will. If you choose your own will, you will soon experience disappointment, because you are attempting to climb the mountain of life relying on your own limited strength, your own ideas, resources, and dreams. Sooner or later you will find yourself leading a humdrum existence characterized by boredom, weariness, a feeling that you are getting nowhere, and, at times, despair.

Your life will be dull, even though you try to make it interesting, and deep down inside you will never be satisfied. Admit it; you cannot deny it.

Finally, at the end of your life, you will die without leaving a trace. Just a few tears and then, inevitable, total oblivion.

If, instead, you choose to do God's will, with your life you will be repeating Jesus' words: *"Not my will but yours be done."*

For a moment, let us imagine God like the sun. The rays of the sun reach out and touch each one of us, a different ray touching each person. Each ray is God's will for that particular person.

Christians, and all people of good will, are called to move ever closer to the sun by walking in the light of their ray which is unique and distinct from all the others. By doing so, they fulfill the particular and wonderful plan which God has for them.

If you also do the same, you will find yourself involved in a divine adventure beyond your wildest dreams. You will be both actor and spectator in something great that God is accomplishing in you and—through you—in humanity.

Everything that happens to you: joys and sufferings, blessings and misfortunes, significant and insignificant events alike—from success and good fortune to accidents and the death of loved ones; and even your everyday activities at home, school, or work—will acquire new meaning, because they come to you from the hand of God who is love.

All that happens is willed or permitted by him for your good. Even if at first you accept this only through faith, later you too will see that there is a golden thread, as it were, running through the events and circumstances of your life, weaving them together into one beautiful design—God's plan for you.

Does this prospect appeal to you? Do you sincerely want to give a deeper meaning to your life? Then listen. First of all I will tell you *when* to do God's will. Just think for a moment:

the past is gone and you cannot run after it; you can only leave it to God's mercy. The future is not here yet—you will live it when it becomes present. Only the present is in your hands. In the present you have to live the words: *"Not my will but yours be done."*

When you are travelling—and life is also a journey—you usually remain in your seat. It would certainly never cross your mind to start walking up and down the aisle in order to get to your destination sooner. Yet this is what those people do who live their lives dreaming of a future which is not yet here, or thinking of a past which will never return.

No, time moves forward on its own. We must remain steadfast in the present and, in due course, we will reach the fullfillment of our life here on earth.

You will now ask me: how do I distinguish God's will from mine? It is not difficult to distinguish God's will from your own if you remain in the present. I will tell you one way to do it. God speaks within you. Perhaps in the past, his voice has too often been suffocated by you and is now barely audible. But try to listen. God speaks to you. He will tell you when it is the moment to study, when it is the moment to help a friend in need, or to work, or to overcome a temptation or to fulfill one of your duties as a Christian or as a citizen. The voice of God within you urges you to listen to those who speak to you in his name; it helps you face difficult situations courageously.

Don't silence this voice—it's the most precious treasure you possess. Follow it faithfully.

Then, moment by moment, you will construct the story of your life, a story which will be both human and divine because you will have done it in collaboration with God. And you will see wonderful things happen. You will see what God can do in a person who says with his or her whole life, *"Not my will but yours be done."*

Chiara Lubich

You have washed the hands of Jesus

My sister-in-law was in the hospital and I visited her from time to time. In the same room there was an old lady left entirely to herself. Nobody listened to her. One of the first times I was there she started calling me. I started towards her but everybody, including my sister, tried to advise me, saying: "Don't pay any attention to her; she's an old woman, a bit crazy, and does that all day long."

A little embarrassed, I was about to sit down when I remembered the Word of Life. It was as if a voice inside was telling me: "Go and do what you are asked." I got up and approached the old lady, barely overcoming a certain repulsion because her hands were very dirty. I did what she asked me and went to fetch a basin of water so she could wash herself. After washing herself she touched my arm and said: "Thank you. You have washed the hands of Jesus."

I was stunned, but I felt a tremendous joy within me, and the confirmation of the certainty that Christ is present in each human being. Ever since that day I try to be at his disposal every time I can.

M.M.

Ann is a young laboratory assistant at the hospital whom I met when she had a medical check-up in the department of preventive medicine where I work. She was then awaiting her first child with such joy, such gentleness that it touched me.

A few months later, I was helping in the pediatric intensive care room. I was taking care of a small girl whose pallor worried me. She was very beautiful but very thin and there was life only in her eyes. I looked at the name, and saw that it was Ann's baby girl.

I paid particular attention to this little girl, and afterwards I met her mother. I tried to cheer her up, to reassure her, to encourage her. She was distraught because of her suffering.

On Christmas night I came to the hospital to see her.

A few days later the child had to be given several blood transfusions and all feeding was stopped because she was allergic to milk and her alimentary canal was severely inflamed. She was getting worse. I thought of baptism. I was about to do it myself, there in the pediatric ward, with the simple gestures any Christian can do, but I said to myself that I had to have the parents' consent, since I had a relationship with the mother.

I asked Ann if the child had been baptized. She answered that they had intended to do it when she got better, but they could not do it in the hospital.

I explained to her that she herself could baptize her so as to give the child every chance, every possible grace for these difficult moments.

She confided to me how distressed she was because the child was in danger of death, and how she prayed to God, making vows, offering everything.

At this moment, I felt moved to tell her to give her child to God, to have full confidence in him, and to adhere completely to his will for her little daughter. He could take her back to him, or save her, but she belonged to him. Ann said yes.

A short time later, she told me she had baptized the little girl and that she was continuing moment by moment to give her to God and to place herself in God to save the child, confident, even if the child was getting worse. Together we prayed that the child would be healed.

A month and a half ago, in the supermarket, I saw Ann coming towards me. She threw her arms around me, beside herself with happiness: "The baby is cured, I am taking her home!" I cried for joy with her.

Later she came to see me and said: "This trial has been an extraordinary grace, a miracle, not only because the child is cured (medically speaking, there had been no hope) but also for my husband and I. We did not really know each other. I discovered that my husband had a deep faith which became stronger on account of this trial; now our relationship is on another level, based on the essential."

F.N.

STARTING FROM SCRATCH

This summer I worked as a prospector in the Alps. This work is done in teams of two and I had the "luck" to team up with Christiane. I say "luck" because the Word of Life was: "Not my will but yours be done."

Each morning, getting up to leave for the mountain, my only desire was to send Christiane about her business alone on account of her behavior the day before. In my view, she really had a bad temper, a little too much for my little life to endure. I wanted to have a quiet three months. I kept telling myself: "It's her fault, it's up to her to be nicer...." But there was also that small voice telling me each morning: "Start from scratch and love Christiane more than yesterday."

For a month and a half there were ups and downs: day by day I tried to do my part to build our life together, and harmony grew. Yet I knew it could all be destroyed by an impulsive act.

One week we had to sleep in the same hotel room. Christiane is a light sleeper and I make a bit of noise during the night. For five days, she barely slept. On the sixth morning, we took the car to go up the mountain. She was driving in a nervous, erratic fashion. At one point we just missed a farm wagon and found ourselves going 60 km per hour across a recently mowed field. Remaining calm and seeing that she was keeping her foot on the accelerator because of the shock, I whispered in her ear after 300 meters: "If you want, we can stop...." Immediately, I promised myself in my heart not to judge this "fault." I took the wheel and the day went on.

During the final week, as we were writing up our report, I called the parents of my best friend, Yves—and learned that he had been killed in the mountains. Right away I called a close friend, told him the news, cried a little, and entrusted Yves as well as his whole family to God. And from that moment on, day by day an extraordinary adventure began with Yves: he became more and more present and alive. With Christiane, that day, everything changed. Everything I had been doing for her until then, she did for me during that last week. Even doing the report, for instance, she read me what she was writing to see if I agreed.

Christiane was able to overcome her character, while I was able to go beyond my little hasty and limited judgments. The work became a common task with a simple team spirit.

Jill

THE WARNING SIGNAL

I had to go away for one day, to take part in a meeting—on Mother's Day. My wife and I had discussed it together. Everything seemed okay and I would be free to go that day. On several occasions, however, I perceived in my children and my wife a certain discontent, and within me a warning signal sounded: perhaps this was the moment to live the Word.

From that moment on, I detached myself from this meeting and started to live for Mother's Day—i.e. living for my wife both in our exchanges during the day, and in choosing the gift with the children. I wanted that day to be ideal, totally dedicated to my wife. So I stayed with her all the time, giving her a hand in dishwashing, cleaning, and various household chores. Naturally, she was a bit surprised to see me always with her, but I told her that it was my surprise way to live Mother's Day, really sharing the time together. I wanted to live for her. And we did everything together, all day long; it was marvelous. She was very happy, and so were the children and I.

As the day unfolded, I often remembered that what was important was to be present—but really present, in body and spirit: attentive, discreet, sensitive, ready for anything.

R.S.

TIME IS TOO PRECIOUS TO WASTE

Two weeks ago, I had an automobile accident on the highway while driving to work. The car I was cautiously driving skidded across the highway on account of the rain. The oncoming cars succeeded in avoiding a collision with me. Only a truck blew a tire as it suddenly turned aside.

It is difficult to describe what I experienced during that uncontrollable trajectory, during the eternity the side-slip lasted. First, an immense joy because I had arrived at the end, at the goal; and then, simultaneously, the anguish of not being able to add anything to what had been my life, of not being able to start over again. When the car stopped just before smashing under the truck, just before the end I thought inevitable, a wave of disappointment came over me. But immediately afterward I was filled with indescribable relief: I would be able to love again, to go forward with each new day, striving toward an ideal of life capable of bringing me and all who live it to a fuller life, greater holiness.

Looking back, I see that since that day something new has come into my life, almost without my being aware of it; that is, a deeper commitment to live fully everything that life brings my way. And on a more intimate level, I feel I have lost that little part of me that I was still keeping for myself just so I could be "me": sometimes happy, sometimes sad, disconcerting, unpredictable, different—in other words, myself. As if "being myself" was a right I could not deny myself.

But now things have changed. Time is too precious to be wasted just because of my changeable moods. I have turned over a new leaf. Now I feel compelled to love in every moment, completely, forever, and with no second thoughts.

C.C.

A COMPLETELY NEW STRENGTH

We got to know a couple, Peter and Mary, who were married nine years ago and have two children. The couple was on the verge of splitting up. They no longer could bear each other and Mary had already told her husband that she had decided to ask for a legal separation. Peter tried to persuade her not to, but to no avail. It was at this point that he asked us to help.

He recognized that his behavior towards his wife had been absurd and aggressive and he promised to change. But she did not believe in his promises and remained firmly determined to see a lawyer. At this stage we made a last attempt with Mary, trying to make her understand that she had to give Peter a last chance to change. At first she did not want to listen to our arguments, but later, remembering the Word of Life we had given her some time ago, she made a genuine interior conversion and understood that now was the time for her to put it into practice by starting to be the first one to love.

She began to live the Word of Life intensely, and after a lapse of nine years, started to go to mass and communion again. She experienced a completely new strength and wanted to share it with her husband; but she understood that, above all, she had to respect his freedom.

Not long afterward, Peter came to see us and said that he would gladly start going to church again, but that he was in the same situation as his wife had been because, like her, he had abandoned religion after their wedding. We encouraged him a bit and he decided to return to the sacraments and to go to the Christmas midnight mass.

That mass was truly a mass of thanksgiving. We met them there, and Peter admitted that he had never had such a Christmas.

Now they give all their friends the Word of Life, telling them their experience because, they say, their marriage has never been so beautiful and authentic.

A.Z.

6

A question of faithfulness

"Whoever is faithful in small matters will be faithful in large ones." (Lk 16:10)

Have you ever felt in your heart the desire to accomplish great things? You must have.

Have you ever felt attracted to people—like heroes or saints—who were able to step out of the ordinary and accomplish important and noble works worthy of admiration? Again, the answer is probably yes, for these aspirations are common to every human being because, as human beings, we all have a great destiny.

Unfortunately, however, most people are incapable of fulfilling their destiny because they are unable to find a way to cope with the more decisive and difficult moments in life.

If you don't mind, I will suggest to you a way to be prepared for those moments.

Jesus had this to say: *"Whoever is faithful in small matters will be faithful in large ones."*

This saying existed before Christ and was probably a proverb. Jesus made use of it in his teaching, giving it a new meaning. We find these words in the Gospel of Luke in a passage where Jesus speaks about money. Their first significance, therefore, is economic but they can be applied to countless situations in life. Jesus indicates with these words that faithfulness in small matters is a sure test that a person will be just as faithful in large ones.

Moreover, since Jesus wants us to be faithful in small

matters, then nothing which life demands of us is insignificant. For nothing is small if we do it in order to fulfill his will. Nothing is small if it is done out of love.

"Whoever is faithful in small matters will be faithful in large ones."

How many little things there are in our everyday life! There is the table to clear, that answer to give, that boring, monotonous job which must be finished, that car to drive, that homework to complete, that meal to prepare, that activity to organize, that instrument to play, those clothes to hang up, that paper to pick up, that smile to offer, that article to write, that happy event to share.

How, then, should we perform these little actions?

We must never do things hurriedly, but rather, we must do everything perfectly. We have to project ourselves wholeheartedly into what we have to do.

To be faithful in little things means to live well the present moment of our life.

"Whoever is faithful in small matters will be faithful in large ones."

Yes, in "large" matters, in those crucial situations in life: a serious accident, a natural disaster which you live through, the death of someone dear to you, that success which could go to your head, an inheritance which you didn't expect, a deep and unexpected sorrow, a responsibility suddenly thrust upon you... And in certain nations, all the unforeseen hardships of war.

I will tell you about a twenty-one-year-old Lebanese whose name is Fouad. He had learned well how to love in the everyday situations of life, in the little things. But, not too long ago, something out of the ordinary happened.

On his way back to Lebanon from a convention in Rome, some armed men stopped him on the road to Beirut about three miles from the airport. It was a difficult moment for he was in a Muslim zone. The militants read on his I.D. card "Maronite Christian."

"Yes, I am a Maronite Christian," Fouad said, "and I'm on my way home."

"You're coming with us," they said to him.

Then, they interrogated him. At the end, they told him, "Do you know what is in store for you?" Fouad understood that for him this was the end. One of the militants took him to a bridge where several Christians had already been killed. While walking to the bridge, Fouad tried to remain calm and he thought of what God might want from him in this moment. It was clear that he had to love his neighbor. Therefore he tried to make his captor feel loved. He told him, "Your job must be difficult, depressing... carrying on this war..." As they drew near the bridge, his guard stopped, looked at him and exclaimed, "Let's go back!"

When they reached the headquarters, Fouad saw his guard speaking to the other men. One of them came over to tell him, "You are lucky, because a few days ago, his brother was killed." This was as if to say, "If there were someone who could have a reason to kill you, this would be he."

So Fouad, who had lived before God in all the little events of his life, was able to remain faithful to God in this experience as well.

And God saved him.

Chiara Lubich

The traffic jam

Driving into the city this morning I suddenly found myself hurrying without reason. I had gotten caught in heavy traffic and then, next thing I knew, I was like everyone else: tense, trying not to let anyone get ahead of me, etc. All at once I thought of the Word of Life. And in that moment, in the midst of the bumper-to-bumper traffic, I relaxed: I smiled at someone who turned toward me; I let someone else get ahead of me; I didn't step so hard on the accelerator when a red light turned green. Gradually I began to feel more myself, more in the presence of God, calm and serene. I stopped being concerned about time and was able to concentrate on living the present moment.

Back home this afternoon, I really had a good opportunity to lose my temper: my daughter Mary had me looking for a paper for two hours and then she found it in her own pocket. But I was able to handle the situation with great peace, and I know where that peace came from.

L.P.

A week in the diabetic ward

Sunday

Today I had an idea that might prove useful. It came to my mind because one of the diabetic patients brought in today had apparently not understood the importance of staying on his medicine and his diet, and so he had not taken them seriously. And as a consequence he was back in the hospital. So I thought that we could try running off an information sheet for our patients, describing the characteristics of diabetes and its consequences. I made a first draft and I plan to show it to Dr. M., the head physician in our department.

Monday

Dealing with Dr. M. is certainly not easy. Everyone makes fun of him behind his back because he is such a stickler for order and precision. If anyone makes the least oversight he takes it out on everybody. Today several people were complaining and I was tempted to join in; but I made a positive effort instead to play down their criticism and to be understanding in his regard, just as I would try to be with anyone else.

As for my idea about the diabetes information sheet, I wanted to be ready to lose my own ideas in order to listen to the ideas of the others. And I felt that the first person I should consult was Dr. M. to see what his opinion was. I was afraid he would find fault with it. Instead, he accepted it. And not only did he approve, but he said that it was a very useful initiative that would benefit the patients. Then he gave me some words of encouragement which were quite unexpected—considering that he calls himself an atheist. "Young lady, you've read the Gospel, haven't you? Well then, act immediately on this proposal of yours...."

Tuesday

Yesterday I really made a serious mistake. I was supposed to leave written instructions that one of the patients was to have a test taken; but I completely forgot. Today, when I arrived the nurses and the other personnel on the floor had already been told about it, and they immediately warned me to be prepared for the worst.

As soon as Dr. M. saw me he asked if I knew anything about the test that patient had missed. Without looking for excuses, I replied that it was my fault. He looked me in the eye and with unheard-of consideration he said—almost smiling—that I had really made a serious mistake, but that he understood, and that I should be more careful next time. As for the present situation, he said, we would find a way to compensate for the missed test.

Everyone else was amazed to see such a change in him. I thought to myself that I was getting back what I try to give, because Dr. M. dealt with me this morning in the same way that I have dealt with him so many times.

Wednesday

At work it sometimes happens that I feel ignored and it seems that everyone else is going about their business as if I weren't there at all. This makes me suffer but I don't want to give up. Every one of those minutes can become something precious. I feel that I am the one who must take the first step toward my co-workers in order to build a relationship with them, starting with little things. This morning I bought a cup of coffee for one of them and I helped another to find some records she had lost.

Thursday

Marie· is a difficult person to get along with. She tries in every possible way to cause me problems. She almost neglects her own patients in order to take care of mine and she creates confusion in the whole ward.

Today I got up the courage to tell her that her attitude is wrong because it is harmful to the patients themselves. At first her reaction was negative, but I continued my offensive of love: when I gave her the envelopes containing the test results for her patients, I left them sealed so that she might be the first to know the results; and later I went to call her to participate in a decision that was being made regarding the whole ward, so that she would not feel left out.

Friday

I was asked to give a presentation of a clinical case history to a seminar of university medical students and professors. The idea frightened me at first. After all, I've only just graduated myself, and I'm rather shy... It just seemed somewhat awesome.

Then I remembered that I had once heard Chiara Lubich say that when she was about to receive the Templeton Prize she had been somewhat troubled by the exceptional nature of the event. But then she had thought to herself that, really, the only truly exceptional thing that exists is God. So I understood then that I, too, must do the little things in life as if they were of great importance, and the big things as if they were small, because only the things of God are great. This helped me to put all the things I have to do back in the right perspective.

Saturday

Marie has started speaking to me again. She even suggested that I have my graduation party in her cottage in the country.

The seminar went very well. Dr. M., knowing how I am, couldn't understand how, on a day like today, I could remain so calm and be so much at peace while I was speaking. Jokingly, he asked if I had taken a tranquilizer. Referring to that remark of his the other day, I simply answered: "No, I just reread the Gospel."

A.R.

THE POWER OF THE GOSPEL

This month, for the first time, one of my girlfriends at school gave me the Word of Life. I am just now beginning to live the Gospel, and this month's Word of Life is very well suited to my present situation.

Looking at the kind of life I had been leading at home, I realized that in order to put this Word into practice, I had to change my relationship with my grandmother. I had to show her much more love and understanding. Before, whenever she would ask me something I would never answer more than "yes" or "no." But since I read the Word of Life, each time she has called me I have gone over and sat down beside her and explained to her whatever she wanted to know. I have also shared with her about my life. This little change in me has amazed my mother and the whole family, and I have understood that the little things we do out of love have all the revolutionary power of the Gospel behind them. I am really happy!

F.V.

SOMETHING TO LIVE BY

I gave the Word of Life, "Whoever is faithful in small matters. . . ." to the lady who cleans the classrooms on my floor. I asked her to read it and tell me if she liked it, and to let me know if she wanted to receive the next Word of Life. A few days later she told me: "You can't imagine how important that little sheet of paper was for me! Many times I have looked in the teachers' wastebaskets to see if there might be some magazines there which could give me something to live by. I figured that since you teachers educate children, you must surely read things which teach people how to live. Now I've found what I was looking for! Please keep on giving it to me!

It was like a ray of sunshine, like an answer to my searching. And now I intend to live it, because I can sense that here is the solution to all my problems."

M.W.
(Germany)

7
God first

"If anyone comes to me without turning his back on his father and mother, his wife and his children, his brothers and sisters, indeed his very self, he cannot be my follower." (Lk 14:26)

What do you think of this?

These words make terrible, drastic, unheard-of demands on us. Yet, Jesus, who said that marriage is indissoluble and commanded us to love everyone, and in a particular way our parents, is now asking us to put in second place all the beautiful affections we have here on earth, lest they become an obstacle to our direct, immediate love for him. Only God could ask so much.

Jesus wants to forcibly detach us from our natural way of living and wants to bind us to himself before anything else so that he can bring about universal brotherhood on earth.

Therefore, wherever he finds an obstacle to his plan, he "cuts," and in the Gospel he speaks, in a spiritual sense, of the "sword."

He calls those who have not known how to love him more than mother, spouse and life itself, "dead." Do you remember the man in the Gospel who asked if he could bury his father before starting to follow Jesus? Jesus answered him, "Leave the dead to bury their dead" (Lk 9:60).

Perhaps you are afraid when confronted with such a demand. Perhaps you would like to relegate these words of Jesus to his own time, or address them only to those called to follow him in a particular way.

You are mistaken. These words hold true in every age, our own as well. They apply to all Christians, including you. In today's world you will find many opportunities to put this invitation of Christ into practice.

Is someone in your family opposed to Christianity? Jesus wants you to bear witness to him or her with your life and, at the right moment, with words, too, even at the cost of being ridiculed or slandered.

Are you a mother whose husband is asking you to have an abortion? Obey God, and not man.

Does somebody want you to join in an activity whose goals are suspicious or even wrong? Break off with him.

Has a relative offered you money obtained illegally? Maintain your honesty.

Does your whole family encourage you to slow down, take it easy and enjoy the many things the world has to offer? Cut with them so that Christ will not withdraw from you.

"If anyone comes to me without turning his back on his father and mother, his wife and children, his brothers and sisters, indeed his very self, he cannot be my follower."

Are you from a family of non-believers? Did the fact of your conversion to Christ provoke division? Don't worry, for this is the result of living the Gospel. Offer God the anguish in your heart for those whom you love, but don't give up.

Did Christ call you to himself in a particular way, and is now the moment when the total gift of yourself demands that you leave father and mother or even your fiancé?

Make your choice. There is no victory without a struggle.

"If anyone comes to me without turning his back on his father and mother, his wife and his children, his brothers and sisters, indeed his very self, he cannot be my follower."

"...indeed his very self..."

Do you live in a place where persecution is a fact and where being a Christian puts your life in danger? Take courage. At times our faith can ask even this. The age of martyrs is never entirely over for the Church.

Each one of us, in the course of our life, will sooner or later have to choose between Christ and everything else in order to remain a real Christian. So your turn will come too.

Don't be afraid. Don't fear for your life. It is better to lose it for God than to lose it forever. Eternal life is a reality.

Don't be afraid for your family, either. God loves them. If you are able to put them after him, some day he will come and call them with the forceful words of his love, and you will help them to become, with you, true disciples of Christ.

Chiara Lubich

I had promised to visit a very lonely and difficult person one evening from seven to eight o'clock, but when I arrived home at 6:30, I found my husband and children delighted to see that their cook and confidante was home at last. My daughter immediately began speaking of the records she had just bought, and wanted me to listen to them. My husband asked me what I intended to prepare for dinner.

I had to disappoint them, by saying that I had to go and see someone and would not be back until after eight o'clock. Excuses on my part; long and disapproving faces on theirs.

I left, but my conscience was not at ease. I asked myself if it was really God's will to "dump" everybody like this for an almost perfect stranger.

And then the Word of Life came back to my mind. I thought that the person who needed me most at that moment was the one who was counting on me (and with whom I had already cancelled a visit once before), and I told myself that if I was "in God" as I visited this person, he would take perfect care of my family in the meantime. I entrusted my husband and children to him and went to love this person, free from any worries.

When I came back, I found the hundredfold! Not one reproach; a dinner prepared rapidly, but eaten in a relaxed atmosphere, everyone conversing peacefully; and then two hours of dialogue with my eldest daughter while listening to her records, talking about her problems and her life. I could even tell them about the solitude of the person I had seen, and they responded to it.

C.P.

FEAR OF MY COLLEAGUES

My friends and I had firmly decided to give the Word of Life to our colleagues at work; but I had only handed it out to a few people—partly because I feared they would not like it, and partly because I had very little confidence in those who worked with me. (As it turned out, however, they were actually looking for something true and meaningful in life.)

It was during a meeting with a university professor that I was forced to shed all these prejudices. Using an appropriate medical image, he said that in their working environments Christians must open up to everyone and not consider the others as though they were in a sort of deep spiritual coma. Furthermore, he added, anyone in any environment can always benefit from hearing a few words from someone who believes.

It was a tough lesson! I remembered all my hesitations and I thought: "It's true. Some day, Jesus, you will remind me of these colleagues and you will ask me: 'What did you do for them?'"

After this examination of conscience I decided to love them in a new way. When I returned to the office, I gave the Word of Life to my other colleagues, no longer afraid of what people might think of me for showing my faith and my convictions so openly. That same day one of them asked to speak with me. He was one of those who was most at odds with the Church. He told me that he had been very happy to read this commentary because it related in a very real way to something that concerned him deeply.

Afterwards, other colleagues also came to tell me the same thing.

N.C.

THE CHOICE

In spite of my desire to go to mass on Sundays, I could never manage to do it. Even though I kept proposing it to my husband and children, they did not want to hear about it and did everything possible to prevent me from going. This made me feel very dissatisfied. Then came the Word of Life, "If anyone comes to me without turning his back on...." One Sunday I felt certain that I had to leave what I was doing at home to go to mass. When I came back, everyone was preparing to go to a show. At that moment, since I had left some work undone, and could not finish everything at once, I said that I was glad to give up the show because, by going to mass, I had chosen what was more important to me. Since that day some of them have started coming with me on Sunday—especially the youngest, who really understood what I meant and who accompanies me now every Sunday.

M.F.

I WAS BORN BEFORE YOU IN CHRIST

When I became an adolescent my father invited me to follow him in his Muslim religion. He told me, "You are my first-born son in whom I have put all my confidence, and you will inherit my power and by my successor." Although I was afraid of offending my father, I answered him: "Father, I started Christianity before you, so even if I am your son, I was born before you in Christ. You follow the way of Muhammad; I follow the way of Christ. I ask you to let me follow the way I have chosen before you, while you follow yours. I know that you love me deeply but under no circumstances will I go back."

I also showed him the parallels between the names one finds in the Koran and in the Bible—like Jesus and Inza, Mary and Miriam, Abraham and Ibrahim. I told him that all the people who had lived on earth were now together in heaven.

My father listened to me with love and left me free to follow my religion. He maintained his affection for me. At the end of his life, he gave the customary paternal blessing for a son who is loved to the end: he breathed and spat in the palm of my hands. I saw that the Holy Spirit had worked in both of us. Fatherly love was burning in my dad and an equally strong filial love was burning in me. The Holy Spirit had helped me to live the word of the Gospel: "If anyone comes to me without turning his back on his father and mother, his wife and his children, his brothers and sisters, indeed his very self, he cannot be my follower."

P.D.
(Ivory Coast)

8
Ask!

"All you ask the Father in my name he will give you." (Jn 15:16)

The most absurd thing in this world is that, on the one hand, there are so many disoriented people endlessly searching for something, anxious for help, and feeling like orphans in the midst of life's inevitable trials; and on the other hand, there is God who is everyone's Father and who would like nothing better than to use his almighty power to grant the wishes of his children and satisfy their needs.

It is like an emptiness and a fullness crying out for each other. Yet the two do not meet. The freedom with which human beings are endowed can produce even this unhappy situation.

But for those who acknowledge him, God never ceases to be Love.

Listen to what Jesus says: *"All you ask the Father in my name he will give you."* This is one of several statements, full of promises, that we find in the Gospels, and through which Jesus teaches us in various ways how to obtain what we need. And it goes without saying that even a blind man could see that this particular Word of Life is God's word.

What great man or woman, what ruler, what mother or father, what person who loves you, even with all his heart, could promise to give you *"all"* you ask?

Only God can speak in this way. His power is unlimited and

he can bestow all graces, whether they be spiritual or material, possible or impossible.

But pay close attention: Jesus tells you *how* to present your request to the Father. *"In my name,"* he says. If you have even a little faith, these three short words should give you confidence. Jesus lived here among us and knows our countless needs, and he feels sorry for us. So when we pray, he wants to be involved. It is as if he were saying to each one of us: "Go to the Father on my behalf and ask him for this and that and the other thing." He knows that the Father cannot say "No" to him because he is his son and he is God.

You do not go to the Father on your own behalf, but on behalf of Christ. You become simply his messenger. It is Jesus who takes care of the matter with his Father.

There are many Christians who pray in this way and who could tell you of the innumerable graces they have received which show that, in his fatherly love, God watches over them every day.

"All you ask the Father in my name he will give you."

You may say to me. "I have asked time and again in the name of Christ but to no avail."

That is possible. I mentioned before that there are other passages of the Gospel in which Jesus invites us to ask for what we need. In them he gives further explanations which you have probably overlooked.

He says, for instance, that we obtain what we request if we "remain" in him, and that means to remain in his will.

God has a marvellous plan for each one of us, and also for you. It is composed of thousands and thousands of situations, events, encounters, people and things. It is a plan born of the highest and most sublime love. Therefore, once we have discovered that God is our Father, the most intelligent thing we can do is live the rest of our lives following not our own will, but God's will, moment by moment.

Suffering is not excluded from his plan for us, precisely because it is a plan of love, and because suffering is an essential and meaningful element in the life of a Christian. Suffering brings about spiritual purification and patience, and nurtures all the virtues. Through your suffering you help Christ to redeem the world.

It is possible that you may ask for something which doesn't coincide with God's plan for you, something which he doesn't consider useful to your life here on earth or in heaven, or which he even considers harmful. How could he, your Father, grant your prayer in this case? He would be betraying you, and that he will never do.

Therefore, it might be useful for you to make an agreement with him before praying, and to say: "Father, I would like to ask you this in Jesus' name if you think it is okay." If the grace you are asking is in harmony with God's loving plan for you, then you will see the truth of the words "All you ask the Father in my name he will give you."

It could also be that you ask for graces without any intention of conforming your life to what God demands. Do you think that in this case it would be fair for God to grant what you request? He doesn't want to give you only a gift; he wants to give you complete happiness, and you can possess it only if you live the commandments of God, and his words. It is not enough to think about them, or even to meditate on them; they must be lived.

If you do this, you will obtain everything.

To summarize, would you like to obtain graces?

Ask for anything you want in the name of Christ, intending, above all, to do his will and obey his laws.

God is very happy to give us graces. Unfortunately, we seldom give him the chance.

Chiara Lubich

The key

This evening I went to dinner with friends. Coming back I remembered I had forgotten the key. I was afraid the door would be locked and that I would have to wake someone up in order to enter. But I remembered that what was important was to do everything for God: It was what I had tried to live during the day. So I prayed to the Lord, as a child to his Father. When I arrived, the door was not locked!

C.P.

The hidden shoes

One of my friends had asked me to pick up her son's pair of shoes. He needed them for the next day, Sunday, his birthday. I promised to do it as soon as possible. But I was unable to fetch them during the day on account of my chores, and when I saw evening coming on, I ran to reach the store before closing time.

It was not yet 7 p.m. but no one was there. What could I do? I decided to ring the bell of the house next door. An old lady opened. I explained my situation to her, and asked what I could do. By chance, it turned out that she was the mother of the people who look after the store. She said that her children had left and live outside the town. I asked her if it was possible to call her daughter, and she agreed to do me that favor. She had trouble with the phone so I helped her dial the number. Her daughter did not seem to be very happy to hear that I was alone with her 82 year-old mother. I had put myself in a delicate situation, so I tried to be as pleasant as possible, hoping she would tell me where the shoes were. Nothing of the sort: she hung up saying, "If you can find them, take them."

We both searched every corner, without luck. What would my friend say? Then, I thought of the Word of Life: "Father, in the name of Jesus, we need these shoes. They are for you, you need them." The grandmother could not do more than she had already done. As for me, I could not delay any longer. I was about to leave when I saw what might be a package under some papers, and I took it. I knew right away it was the young boy's shoes: the name was written on it. Filled with joy I kissed the old lady and gave her a hug. I was happy and so was she. While I had not lost hope completely, I never thought I would succeed in bringing back the shoes to my girlfriend.

A.F.

IF IT IS HIS WILL

I have a twenty-year-old daughter whose job obliges her to work in the city and come home only one day a week. She became acquainted with a young man. They began going out together, and she thought she loved him. Three months passed. One day, a friend advised me to try to end the relationship because this young man was not fit for her. I went to the city, made my own inquiries, and found that she was right. My husband and I tried to reason with our daughter, but she did not listen to us, because she said she loved him.

I prayed a lot, beseeching God to hear me if it was his will. And I lived the Word of Life as well as I could, trying to do everything out of love.

Five months later, my daughter announced that she had broken off the relationship. I cried from joy and thanked God; and now, I continue to pray for the future of my children.

A mother

THE LOST AND FOUND SON

In the school where I work, a little Arab boy in the sixth grade skipped school for the third time. I went to inform the parents. That same night, the child did not return home. The mother in tears, the father frantic, they searched around town all night, looking for him. In the morning no child; at noon still nothing.

In the afternoon, I had to supervise some children for one hour. I said to myself: "Here I am doing nothing for this family which is heartbroken; I could at least pray...."

I thought of the Word of Life, "All you ask the Father in my name..."; I thought of Mary who experienced the same anguish when Jesus, as a child, had been lost in the temple. Praying was the only thing left for me to do.

As I watched the students I start praying with all my strength: "Lord, do something...."

At the end of the school day, I went out and saw in the distance the weeping mother approaching. What could I tell her? We had no news.

Then the miracle happened. On my left, an employee of the school approached, holding by the hand the lost and now found child: "I have just found this child in the passageway near the kitchen." Deeply moved, I gave the child to his mother, who could not believe her eyes. As she was about to leave, I said to her with all my heart, *"El hamdoullah!"*— "Thanks be to God!"

G.M.
(France)

Three children tell this story.

"One day, we were looking at television when our mother came to tell us that a six-year-old girl friend of ours had been rushed to the hospital for appendicitis, and that she had to be operated on. So all together we recalled the Word of Life and prayed to God in the name of Jesus for the success of the operation.

"The same evening, we learned that our friend had suddenly stopped crying, had started to play in her bed, and that when the doctor came to operate on her, he had said that it was no longer necessary, even though it would have to be done later.

"We asked the mother of our friend at what time she stopped crying. It was just at the moment of our prayer. It made us very happy to see that God had heard us and that if he knows a thing is good for us, he gives it to us."

9
Keep watch

"Keep watch, because you do not know on what day your Lord will come." (Mt 24:42)

Have you noticed that often your life just drags on because you are not living it fully but are waiting for "tomorrow," in anticipation of something "beautiful" you hope it will bring?

There is, indeed, a "beautiful tomorrow" in store for you, but it is not the one you expect.

A God-given instinct leads you to look forward to something or someone that will be able to satisfy you. You look forward to a holiday celebration, a vacation, or some special encounter; but then when everything is over you are not satisfied, or not fully satisfied. And you start the routine of your life again without conviction, always looking forward to something else.

The truth is, that among the many elements in human life there is one that no one, including you, can escape—the face-to-face meeting with the Lord who is coming. This is the "beautiful tomorrow" you are unconsciously looking for, because you are made for happiness, and only he can give you full happiness.

Jesus knows how you and I search for happiness blindly; therefore, he warns us: *"Keep watch, because you do not know on what day your Lord will come."*

With these words, Jesus is speaking of his coming on the last day. As he ascended into heaven from among the apostles, so will he return. But these words also refer to the coming of the Lord at the end of each person's life. After all, when a person dies, for him or her the world is ended.

Since you don't know if Christ will come today, tonight, tomorrow, or in a year or more, you must be vigilant. You must be as those who keep watch because they know the thief is coming but don't know the hour.

Be vigilant, be alert, be awake because there are many things that you can have doubts about on earth, but one thing is certain—some day you will die. This, for a Christian, means to meet Christ who is coming.

Perhaps, like many others, you try to forget about death. You fear that moment and live as if it were never going to come. Rooting yourself more and more in this earthly life, you say, "Death frightens me; therefore it doesn't exist." Yet that moment will come because Christ will certainly come. *"Keep watch, because you do not know on what day your Lord will come."*

If Jesus is coming, then this life is a passing thing. But that does not mean that you should undervalue it. On the contrary, you should give it the highest importance. You must prepare yourself for that encounter with him by living a worthy life.

On the morning of August 6, 1978, Pope Paul VI didn't know and maybe didn't even imagine that that night at 9:40 the Lord would come. But he was ready. In his more recent talks he had often mentioned his impending death. He had prepared himself and, therefore, his sudden death didn't take him by surprise. For John Paul I, the coming of Jesus was even more unforeseeable.

"Keep watch, because you do not know on what day your Lord will come."

You, too, must be vigilant. Your life is not merely a peaceful chain of events; it is also a struggle. And a wide variety of temptations, such as those regarding sexuality, vanity, attachment to money, and violence, are your first enemies.

If you are always vigilant you won't be taken by surprise. Those who love are always vigilant. Vigilance is a characteristic of love.

When you love someone you are constantly watching and waiting for him or her to come. Every moment away from the one you love is spent with him or her in mind.

For instance, a wife whose husband is away thinks of him as she goes about her work or as she prepares something for him. Everything is done with him in mind. Consequently, when he arrives at the end of the day she is overjoyed to see him.

Similarly, when a mother is caring for a sick child her thoughts are with him even as she rests.

In the same way a person who loves Jesus does everything with him in mind, encountering him in the simple expressions of his will in every moment, and preparing for that solemn encounter with him on the day when he comes.

It was November 3, 1974. At Santa Maria in southern Brazil a religious convention for 250 young people had just ended. Most of them had come from the city of Pelotas. The first chartered bus left with 45 people who were joyfully singing. As they were traveling, some of the girls started to pray the sorrowful mysteries of the rosary, asking Our Lady to help them to be faithful to God to the end of their lives. A short time later, the brakes failed and the bus went out of control around a curve, turning over three times as it fell 150 feet. Six girls died. One who survived said, "I saw death but I was not afraid because God was there." Another one said, "When I realized I could move, I knelt in the midst of the debris among the bodies of my friends, and I looked at the starry sky and prayed. God was there with us."

The father of Carmen Regina, one of the girls who died, said that she used to say: "Dying is a beautiful thing, Dad, because you go to be with Jesus."

"Keep watch, because you do not know on what day your Lord will come."

The girls of Pelotas loved, and because they loved they were vigilant; and when the Lord came, they went to meet him joyfully.

Chiara Lubich

THE RIGHT MOMENT

It was the end of my shift. I had already worked hard (eight deliveries). A woman arrived. She was just starting to have contractions and all was going well with her and for the child she carried.

I had her put to bed, thinking that she would give birth in about two hours and that since my shift ended in thirty minutes, my replacement would look after her.

Fifteen minutes later, as I was passing her door, the "voice" inside me told me to go and see her. There was no apparent reason for doing so (at that stage of labor I check only every hour); but I felt that I had to listen to that voice. So I offered that moment to God, entered, and, since I was there, I examined the woman. At that very moment an extremely dangerous situation was developing for the child—one that would bring death in a matter of minutes if nothing were done. The umbilical cord, the unborn infant's only source of oxygen, had become wedged in front of the child's head, which was pressing against it, thus interrupting the circulation.

With my fingers I pushed back the baby's head and at the same time discreetly signalled for help. Five minutes later, a perfectly healthy baby girl was delivered by Caesarian section.

As we came out of the operating room, the obstetrician said, "I cannot understand how you happened to be there at the right moment." Then I gave him the Word of Life.

On my next shift, I saw the mother again. She was now aware of what had happened and she asked me the same question, so I gave her the Word of Life too. She was very happy. She does not believe in God, but she told me: "I will always keep this because I want my daughter to know some day that she owes her life to this sentence of the Gospel."

C.C.

IN THE WAITING ROOM

A few days ago, a person asked the surgeon with whom I work for the results of his father's tests. The results were terrible; they showed a malignant tumor. An operation would be attempted but probably nothing could be done.

The man became pale. His mother and sister were waiting for him outside. How could he give this news to them? How could he tell his father? He seemed desparate.

I felt that his suffering was mine. I approached him and asked, "Do you believe in God?"

He lifted his head and looked at me, bewildered. "Yes, of course, in a certain way I believe in Him."

The surgeon, who had already left, was calling me so I had to leave. But a few minutes later, as I was passing through the waiting room again, I saw that he was still there thinking, with his head in his hands.

I always have a few copies of the Word of Life in my handbag. I took one and gave it to him. A little surprised, he started reading: "Keep watch, because you do not know on what day your Lord will come."

I tried to explain to him: "In this suffering, it is really God who is coming to you with all His love. . . ." He listened to me attentively and seemed to find some peace in what I said.

As he was leaving, he suddenly turned toward me and said, "I would appreciate it if you would be present during the operation. Your presence would give us courage."

On the morning of the operation I was there, praying to Jesus that I would be only an instrument of His love.

L.F.

The light of the Word

Tuesday, November 28th

In today's mail I received a letter from my parents informing me that my uncle is in the hospital and that they are at his side. But the letter was eight days old on account of the strike. I immediately called the hospital and spoke with my aunt. She told me that a last-chance operation was about to take place but there was little hope. Without hesitating, I assured her that I would be with them for the weekend.

I then found myself alone with my memories. My uncle was always ready to do anything for us when I was a child...But the years have flown by. We now live hundreds of miles apart and I have seen little of him lately. Spontaneously, I prayed that he would not leave us this time, because I have not loved him very much and maybe it isn't too late.

Wednesday, November 29th

I received a phone call from my sister. She told me that my uncle did not survive the operation. I called my cousin and arranged to join him in Paris. Saturday morning we will go together to see his father.

Friday, December 1st

At 7:30 a.m. I was at the Austerlitz station on my way to meet my cousin. But I felt I had little to offer him. I have a friend who lives near the station so I called him and he invited me for breakfast. Before I left to meet my cousin, my friend and I read the Word of Life for the month: "Keep watch, because you do not know on what day your Lord will come." The recent events had made me more responsive to this phrase and I tried to make it mine. I then went to meet my cousin. His two-year-old son was there. The child's presence and cheerfulness reminded us that life is stronger than death; there was no need for words.

During the trip I learned a few things about my uncle. Just before his operation he had asked the family to lend his records to a particular neighbor whom he used to visit every week. This person had had a leg amputated and, since my uncle could not listen to his records in the hospital, he thought his friend could enjoy them. Up until they took him to the operating room he tried to smile and joke with everyone. He was a real comedian. And even when they tried to assure him that after the operation everything would be fine again, he nodded and went along with them, for the last time, out of love for all of them.

When we arrived, most of my immediate family was there, as well as my retired uncles and their children. My aunt reminded me that she and my uncle had become inseparable, especially since their retirement. We never saw one without the other.

Saturday, December 2nd

I was asked to do one of the readings during the mass; I went to see the priest to arrange it. I explained to him that certain members of my family have a weak faith, if they still have any faith at all. I also told him who my uncle was and how he was appreciated in the neighborhood. He suggested that I say a few words after the first reading. I was a bit apprehensive about doing this; I feared it would be ill-received. But the message from the Word of Life again gave me light: "Keep watch...." When the time came, I said, "If I

112

read this passage from St. Paul, it is because I, too, believe with him that in Christ those who love will also be reborn...."

Later someone told me that he had appreciated what I said. Beyond the words, something had happened.

After the burial, everyone surrounded my aunt. I felt that these two intense days—and the others that had led up to them—had washed away years of misunderstanding with certain members of my family, due to my choice of God.

I also felt that among everyone present the love that bound them to my uncle had been stronger than anything else.

J.V.

A VIGILANT LOVE

I was new in the bank, in a department in which I never worked before. It was difficult for me, in spite of my enthusiasm, because nobody was training me. Nobody, that is, except one employee with whom I had to work a lot. Little by little he spoke about his family; he was in the process of getting a divorce. Since he knew I had gone through a similar situation at home, it seemed that he placed importance in what I could tell him. However, I knew that only one thing could lead him beyond my own limited experience, and so I spoke about his wife and of the suffering she was probably going through. Perhaps he had not thought about that, since often in this type of situation, one tends to count the mutual wrongs instead of looking for reasons for indulgence and understanding.

As the court date approached, I saw him thinking about it, aware that it could be either the occasion to confirm their separation or to start an understanding dialogue. We were working more and more in silence. I had expressed my own deep conviction—that only the will to love one another could help them discover the basis for a constructive solution, one which would be a positive step toward their future.

The day after their reconciliation, he greeted me in the office with a radiant smile. "Guess what happened! I saw my wife and tonight we are getting together." Joy illuminated his face, but I felt that I had been simply a very small intermediary. It had been the power of love, which, in spite of everything else, had breached the wall of legal proceedings that only a few weeks before had threatened to divide them permanently.

C.M.

THE MERCHANT'S TRICK

For the last few months an old relative of mine has been coming over occasionally in the evenings to visit my little business and to talk—"to pass the time a little," as he says. He has been a bit depressed, and I did not enjoy his visits. I even used to keep him standing so that he would leave sooner.

One evening, for the hundredth time, I saw him enter. The first thing that came to my mind was the Word of Life. Right away, I surprised myself by offering him a chair. We then spoke together for a while.

Since that day he has continued to come but he often leaves happier. And thanks to the Word of Life, I never let him go without having given him a little warmth, a smile, that little somethig which may be the *last* act of love I'll do for the *last* neighbor I'll ever meet.

N.I.

10

At the service
of one another

"Put your gifts at the service of one another, each in the measure he has received." (1 Pt 4:10)

Pina, a young woman from Sardinia who has been blind from birth, lives in an institution for the blind. Recently, the chaplain became paralyzed and could no longer celebrate mass. Because of this, it was decided that the Eucharist could no longer be kept in the chapel. When Pina heard this, she asked the Bishop to let them keep the Eucharist—the only light in their darkness—in that home. He granted her request and also gave her permission to distribute Communion to the chaplain and other residents.

In her desire to help others, Pina has also taken on the responsibility of preparing a radio program which is broadcast a few hours every week. She uses this program to share with those who are suffering the best that she has to offer—advice, sound thinking, and the explanation of moral issues—in order to give them strength. I could tell you much more about her. She is blind, but suffering has given her light.

I could give you so many other examples! There is goodness in the world which often goes unnoticed. Pina lives her Christianity: she knows that each of us has received gifts from God and she has put hers at the service of others.

Yes, because the word "gift" (or "charism" as it is derived from the Greek) does not refer only to those graces which God gives those who govern his Church.

Nor does it refer only to those extraordinary gifts which

117

God gives directly to individual Christians for the good of all when they are needed to solve a particular problem in the Church, or in times of serious danger—when the existing institutions are not sufficient. Such gifts include wisdom, knowledge, the power to work miracles, the gift of tongues, the charism to generate a new spirituality in the Church, and so on.

These are not the only gifts or charisms which exist; there are other, more ordinary ones which many people possess and which are noticeable because of the good they bring others. The Holy Spirit is always at work.

Furthermore, natural talents can also be considered gifts or charisms. Therefore, everyone is gifted; you, too.

How should you use these gifts? Try to make them bear fruit. They were not given to you for your own benefit alone but, rather, for the good of all. *"Put your gifts at the service of one another, each in the measure he has received."*

There is a great variety of gifts. Each person has his or her own, and, therefore, each one also has a specific role to fulfill in the community.

Tell me something: what gifts do you have? Do you have a degree? Did you ever think, for instance, of setting aside a few hours each week to teach those who need help, those who cannot afford to pay for their studies?

Are you a very generous person? Did you ever think of getting together with other people of good will in order to help the poor and the outcasts of society? By doing this, you could bring back to many hearts the true sense of human dignity.

Do you have a knack for music, poetry or drama? Did you ever think of making your parish gatherings more beautiful, interesting, and modern, in order to do away with the idea that the liturgy is dull, outdated and somber?

Are you able to comfort others? Are you good at housekeeping, cooking, sewing clothes, or at doing crafts? Look around to see who might need your help.

It pains me to see that many people are bored because they don't know what to do with their free time. We Christians do not have free time—not as long as there are on this earth the sick, the hungry, the imprisoned, or the ignorant, the uncertain, the unhappy, the addicted, the handicapped, the orphaned, the widowed.

And think of prayer. It is such a powerful gift that we can use at any time, since in each moment we can turn to God who is present everywhere. In this regard, I would like to remind you that, in January, a week is set aside during which Christians all over the world pray to God for perfect unity among the Churches. You, too, should try to do your part.

"Put your gifts at the service of one another, each in the measure he has received."

Can you imagine what the Church would like if all Christians, children as well as adults, shared with others the graces they have received? Their mutual love would become so real, so abundant and so striking that non-Christians would be able to recognize them as true disciples of Christ. And that is not all. It would be such a striking witness that no longer could anyone doubt the divinity of Jesus.

If this is going to be the outcome, don't you think you ought to do all you can to bring it about?

Chiara Lubich

An ordinary adventure

I was driving in a snow storm, immersed in my own thoughts, with the heater on high, protected from the cold and the exterior world. I was irritated. After a difficult discussion with a friend I had realized that wounds I thought were healed were, in fact, still open.

A snow-covered hitchhiker was making tired signals to the onrushing vehicles. I was in a bad mood and was not in the proper lane to pick him up, but at that moment I thought of the Word of Life. I did have two gifts to share—first, I knew how to drive and, second, I had a car. Should I put these at his service? Why not? I quickly moved into the right-hand lane and stopped to let the passenger in.

An ordinary adventure: No doubt. But if it had not been for the Word of Life, I would not have lifted my little finger to put those meager gifts at the service of that person.

J.R.

A successful goal

One day when I was playing soccer with friends, the goalie I had chosen let in a stupid goal. Instead of telling him off, as I would have normally done, I went over and explained to him what to do to stop the ball. He was a bit surprised to see my reaction, but he listened and seemed to understand. As a matter of fact, he immediately started playing better. And I was happy because when I started to play I had in mind this Word of Life, which tells us to share our gifts and capabilities.

J.C.

HOUR BY HOUR

Six o'clock

The alarm clock rang right in the middle of a dream! Well, it's a brand new day and there are a lot of things to be done... I get up as quietly as possible; in half an hour I'll be ready and I can wake up the rest of the house by singing a song—my way of ringing the alarm.

Eight o'clock

After half an hour on the subway, I have to cross a large park to get to class. This is my chance to get some fresh air and spend a quarter of an hour with Mary, asking her to be present at every moment of my day.

Ten o'clock

The lecture hall was noisy. All I could do was try to love the unfortunate professor and resist the temptation to join the others in making paper airplanes. Now, in physics, I can at least put one of my gifts at the service of others, by explaining to one of my classmates how a hydraulic pump works. (It's not easy to be patient when you start to feel hungry.)

Noon

In the university cafeteria I get acquainted with a young Muslim girl and she explains to me how she tries to live her faith in Paris among the students. We both feel enriched because our time together has been based on the God in whom the two of us believe.

Two o'clock

I'm reviewing for the oral exam I must take this afternoon. I keep thinking of Antoine, a three-year-old boy who went to heaven not long ago. He must be having a good laugh seeing how distracted I am in my review, so I try to concentrate to show him my good will.

Four o'clock

The assistant who has to give me the exam is there only for me, so I must also be there only for him. It's certainly not my moment of glory, but I try to be honest and not deceive the examiner. In any case, my final Examiner will not ask me what grade I got on this oral test, but how I lived it.

Six o'clock

I met a blind man in the subway and I was able to guide him a little. But, next time, I must be more sensitive in helping a blind person and not ask if he knows where he is going—of course he knows!—but simply put my gift of sight at his service.

Eight o'clock

After mass, Jesus, whom I had just received in the Eucharist, was waiting for me again, sitting on the church steps. This man whom I meet every evening explained to me why he was begging... I invited him to come to mass the next time, before going out to beg, and he said he would. Man does not live on bread alone.

Ten o'clock

Bedtime! I think about this very full day, but also of the gaps I did not fill with love. Tomorrow a new day will begin. I will be able to start all over again....

E.C.

THE MOST BEAUTIFUL CHRISTMAS

We live in a small town, where the pastor who was alone, tired and depressed, no longer had the strength to take care of the parish. For us, living this Word of Life meant putting ourselves at the disposal of our pastor, trying to give him hope, while helping him with his work. We immediately got involved in the parish council, trying to bring in other families we knew.

At Christmas time, we thought of a few projects: prepare the Christmas mass, organize a children's choir, and see who could prepare the best manger scene. We wanted to do everything we could in order to mobilize the families of the parish and create a community around the pastor.

There were difficulties to overcome which were aggravated by the poor health of the parish priest. He did not feel up to celebrating the midnight mass. Moreover, he feared it would be a flop since the last time he had celebrated midnight mass the church had been completely empty. But seeing our good will, he let us go ahead with out plans.

We visited all the families of the parish to bring them greetings on behalf of the pastor, and to tell them of the plans for Christmas. Some offered to help us. A priest who was free for that day even offered his services.

At midnight mass the church was packed. The pastor was happy and deeply moved. Many received communion. The following day the church was again full and the people actively participated in the liturgy. This was repeated on New Year's Day and on the Epiphany.

The pastor said it was the most beautiful Christmas of his life. He wrote an article in the diocesan bulletin saying how happy he was to see the community alive again.

S.R.

FOR THE FIRST TIME

In a little village in northern Italy, 20 persons meet regularly to share how they have lived the Word of Life. "Our mentality is starting to change," they say. "Relationships are growing. We look at one another with new eyes; the old prejudices and grudges tumble down." One of them declares: "In the village it seems as if everything is the same but in reality, between us, everything has changed. Now we love one another. When we meet, a glance is enough to remind ourselves of the Word which is our common bond." And another adds: "I feel that I have discovered the people of my village for the first time. When I think that before I used to meet them every day! Then, I would have never made a sacrifice for someone else, now—yes."

LIKE WILDFIRE

A young couple moved into a house outside of my town that had been abandoned for years. It did not even have running water. They were awaiting the birth of their first child and their relatives did not want to see them anymore. They lived in complete isolation and lacked everything.

The Word of Life, "Put your gifts at the service of one another" made me understand that I could do a lot for them.

I began by gathering together some of the things they needed, first asking my family and friends, and then other people in the town. In just one day this love spread like wildfire between persons who had previously ignored one another. All the couple's necessities were taken care of. There were even those who gave of their time and worked to make the house habitable.

But what is more important, the young couple have found new friends.

M.S.

11

Remain in Christ

"I am the vine and you are the branches; whoever remains in me, with me in him, bears fruit in plenty; for cut off from me you can do nothing." (Jn 15:5)

Imagine a branch cut off from the vine. It has no future, no hope; it is unproductive and there is nothing in store for it but to dry up and be burned.

Think of the spiritual death to which we are doomed as Christians if we do not stay united to Christ. It is a frightening thought: complete sterility—even if we work hard from morning till night, even if we think we are doing good things for humanity, even if our friends applaud us, even if our earthly goods increase, even if we make considerable sacrifices. All this may mean something to us here on earth, but it has no meaning for Christ and for eternity, and that is the life that really matters.

"I am the vine and you are the branches; whoever remains in me, with me in him, bears fruit in plenty; for cut off from me you can do nothing."

How can we remain in Christ and Christ remain in us? How can we be a green and vigorous branch which is fully united to the vine? We must, first of all, believe in Christ. But that is not enough. Our faith must determine how we live our lives. We must, in other words, live in conformity with this faith by putting Jesus' words into practice.

Thus we cannot neglect the divine means—such as the sacraments—which Christ has left us, the means that make it possible for us to obtain that unity with him, or to reacquire it if we have lost it.

Moreover, Christ will not feel that we are solidly united to him, unless we make the effort to be part of our ecclesial community, our local church.

"...whoever remains in me, with me in him, bears fruit in plenty; for cut off from me you can do nothing."

Do you see how Jesus speaks not only of our unity with him, but also of his unity with us? If you are united to him, he is in you; he is present in the innermost part of your heart. And from this comes a rapport, a dialogue of mutual love and a relationship of cooperation between Jesus and you, his disciple. And hence the result: bearing fruit in plenty, exactly as the branch that is solidly united to the vine bears grapes in abundance.

"Fruit in plenty" means that your life will be a fruitful witness to others. You will be blessed with the ability to open the eyes of many to the unique, revolutionary words of Christ, and to give them the strength to follow these words. It also means that in accordance with the gifts God has given you, you will be able to foster or even initiate projects to alleviate some of the sufferings of humanity.

"Fruit in plenty" means fruit in abundance, and this could mean that you will be able to create among those around you an atmosphere of goodness, of mutual love, of true communion.

But *"fruit in plenty"* does not only mean the spiritual and material well-being of others, but your own as well. Your spiritual growth, as well as your personal sanctification depend on your being united to Christ.

Sanctification. Perhaps, in these times of ours, to speak of sanctification may seem anachronistic, pointless, utopian. But it is not. These present times will pass and, with them, all such shortsighted and erroneous views. What will remain is the truth. Two thousand years ago, Paul the apostle said clearly that sanctification is God's will for all Christians. Theresa of

Avila, a doctor of the Church, was certain that everyone can reach the highest contemplation. And the Second Vatican Council declared that all the faithful are called to sanctity.

Work then so that you, too, may gather the "fruit" of sanctity *"in plenty,"* which you can do only if you are united to Christ.

Have you noticed how Jesus is not concerned with the fruit directly, but looks at it only as a result of our remaining united to him?

It might be that some of us fall into the error of many Christians who believe only in activism and more activism—and projects and more projects for the good of others—without taking the time to ask themselves whether they are fully united to Christ. This is a mistake. They think they are bearing fruit, but it is far less than what Christ in them and with them could bear.

If we want to bear fruit that will last and that will have the mark of something divine, we must remain united to Christ; and the more we remain united to Christ, the more fruit we will bear.

The very verb *"remain"* used in this sentence gives you an idea that this bearing fruit, is not a momentary but rather a permanent condition.

If you know people who live this way, you will see, in fact, how even a smile, a word, a simple everyday gesture, an attitude in a given situation enables them to touch other people's hearts even to the point of leading them back to God.

This is the way it was with the saints. But even if we are not saints, we should not get discouraged. All Christians are capable of bearing fruit. Let me tell you a story.

It happened in Portugal. Maria do Socorro had just started college in a very tense environment. Many of the other students were involved in political disputes, each according to his or her own ideology and each trying to win over the students who had not joined any group as yet.

Maria knew what she wanted to do, even though it was not

easy to explain it to her friends. She wanted to follow Christ and to remain united to him. Her companions, however, who knew nothing of her ideas, labeled her wishy-washy, a girl without ideals. At times she felt awkward when they saw her go to church, but she went just the same because she felt she had to remain united to Jesus.

Christmas approached. Maria was aware that among the students there were some who could not go home because they lived too far away. She suggested that the other students get together and give them presents. To her great surprise all agreed right away.

Later there were school elections and another big surprise awaited her: she was elected as representative of her class. Her amazement was even greater, however, when her friends told her that it was only logical that she should have been elected, since she was the only one who followed a precise line of conduct. "You know what you want"—they said—"and how to go about accomplishing it." Now some of them want to find out more about the ideal of her life and to live it with her. This is the fruit of Maria do Socorro's perseverance in remaining united to Jesus.

Chiara Lubich

The clock stood still

I am doing my senior year in mechanical construction, and spend many hours in the workshop working with different machines.

Last Thursday, the eve of the holidays, I had my final session on the lathes. It was 5:00 p.m. and the course would end with the bell at 5:30. Before the bell rang, I had to finish the pieces I had already started, as well as clean and reset the machine. It was difficult to do it all alone in half an hour.

I kept looking at the clock and the three pieces I had to finish. I was getting nervous, and kept telling myself, "You are going to be late and the others are practically finished." And I was wasting a lot of time in uncontrolled, abrupt and nervous movements. So I told myself: "John, what's wrong with you? You must not react this way. Finish this afternoon for Jesus by living each present moment fully. Do everything well and have confidence in him; and you will see, everything will go fine."

As a matter of fact, I then found myself able to work, and the clock almost seemed to stand still. Each time I found myself rushing again, I reconciled things with Jesus so as to do better still.

Then a friend came to help me put the machine in order, and I was able to finish everything on time.

J.S.

Eleven o'clock. In the surrounding streets, ripped-open garbage bags littered the sidewalks, but in front of the ministry the sidewalk was impeccable.

Security guards. Guests. A few dozen journalists waited in silence, each one reading a press release. The others arrived and they formed groups. As for me—I didn't know anyone; at the most I'd be able to put a name on two faces.

A hostess invited us to enter and announced that the Cabinet Minister would be late: he had been detained in Parliament. I felt very small—probably the youngest of the sixty or so people in the hall. Yet, I wanted this moment to be no different from any other: here there were people to be loved, just as much as anywhere else.

The Minister arrived. He sat down at a table, in front of a window through which one could see how magnificent the autumn day was. He began his statement, and I realized that he had nothing new to say on the problem: practically everything was contained in the press release. I was struck by the enormous gap between the real needs of the people which that part of the government is supposed to deal with and the unreal side of this ritual press conference. It hurt me.

But I also saw that here was a man speaking, trying to hold the attention of his audience in spite of the photographers who kept blinding him with their flashes while they moved around noisily. And I realized that the only reason for my being there was to permit him to feel that he was being listened to.

The way I spent that morning may not seem very practical—holding almost no conversation with the journalists, and simply listening to someone. Perhaps. But it was the only way to change the world around me. For a few minutes, I did it quietly.

J.B.

Monday: comprehensive final, part one. The question was simple, but, the fact of the matter was, I didn't know how to answer it. Yes, I had given my studies to you, Lord, telling you that I wanted to lose everything for you. *Saying* it was beautiful! But I never imagined that I would have to accept not being among the first of the class. I never imagined failure. And what about my professional reputation? It will take a beating! I had not foreseen that. However, you are here and I tell you again—since this is the reality I want to live—that whatever you want, I want.

Monday evening. Well I have the results; there's still hope! I have had to lose so much, Lord, during these two years of preparation, in which I have tried to live with you even in school.

Tuesday: part two. Seven candidates were in the room, with two boards of examiners. Six of us waited while one was examined; then another; then another. I was last. I felt as if I had already gone through all six of my predecessors' exams. They knew so much, I almost felt they were my enemies! Enemies? Then I remembered: "If you love only your friends. . ." So I tried to look at them with love. Now what troubles me are those same discouraging thoughts that keep returning: "You're ill-prepared." "You're ignorant." "You barely manage to pass your exams." Lord, I give you all of this, including whatever I have failed to do.

The hardest test is waiting for the results. I passed in everything! The credit, Jesus, goes to you, "the most beautiful of the sons of men," in whom I have believed. I want to remain united to you forever.

C.M.

The Wallpaper

I wanted to make our office more harmonious for the sake of our clients, who range from immigrants in despair to civil servants and well-known local leaders. I discussed it with my colleagues but one of them did not agree. We all dropped the idea, not wanting to act without her. Realizing this, she brought up the question again, explaining that she could not understand why money had to be spent on such a thing when our clients needed something else. I told her that they also needed to feel welcome, to feel loved for themselves, and that the way our office was arranged would help to do that. Suddenly, she understood and agreed.

We went and chose the wallpaper together. She even wanted to buy something a bit more expensive because it was more beautiful.

With such small acts, a bridge has been built between the two of us. As a result, all our work goes much more smoothly.

E.M.

A Memorable Day

Four of us had to leave at 4:15 a.m., to drive to Paris for a meeting. To make it easier, Beatrice and Chantal were going to sleep at my home Saturday night, and we would pick up Gillette as we pased her house in the morning.

Before going to bed, the three of us remembered that the next day daylight saving would begin, and so with one accord we set our watches back one hour—instead of forward!

On Sunday at what I thought was 3:45 a.m., my alarm rang. I got up and was about to wake up Beatrice and Chantal when the phone rang. It was Gillette. "I have been waiting for you for the past two hours. I thought you had forgotten me." I suddenly realized our mistake. We were two hours behind schedule. Gillette said she would come over, while I went to wake the others. It was a race against time! But we had to eat before beginning our 250-mile drive—that was indispensable.

All this could have been a source of tension and bad tempers, but everyone wanted to be a gift for the others, and the departure went smoothly.

As we left the city of Rennes, patches of fog slowed our speed considerably. Where we could have normally done 65 miles per hour, we could not exceed 50; but the joy remained.

About four miles outside Laval, the engine died and we found ourselves beside the road as the day dawned. It was time to live the present moment deeply. We remained calm in the face of this bad luck. A moment later, the motor started again. We searched for a garage and found only a gas station on the edge of Laval. We stopped there, hoping that some competent person would give us a hand. But no, we had to leave after losing a quarter of an hour. The motor seemed to have gone back to normal. I told Jesus: "We are going to Paris for you, so either help us get there without further breakdown—and bring us home too—or help us find a garage that is open, with someone who could repair what is wrong."

Twenty miles outside Mans a garage was open. The mechanic started to work on our motor. Time passed. He took something apart and checked it carefully. The minutes added up.

A motorist arrived, oil dripping from under his car. He was in a nervous state, waiting to see the mechanic who was occupied with our car. We smiled at him and, when he did not respond, we got in our car and started to sing. Our repertoire was pretty well exhausted when at last the car was ready. The motorist was now completely calm, and smiled to see us in such a good mood.

We arrived in Paris at 12:30 p.m., left our car at the Place de l'Italie and took the subway. A few minutes later, a drunken Algerian got on and started to make a scene, shouting loudly, protesting against France and the French. The seats around him emptied. He was striking the subway seats with his fists.

We were scared stiff and began to pray that nothing tragic would happen. Beatrice was facing Chantal. They said to one another that they were ready for whatever Jesus might ask of them in this instant. Then Beatrice began looking at the Algerian without fear and with great love. Their eyes met and, instantly, his anger vanished. He came toward Beatrice to shake her hand, saying, "Forgive me, forgive me."

Our station arrived and he got off the train with us. While going up the stairs toward the square, we shared our few provisions with him: cigarettes, cookies and apples. Our new friend seemed moved by those tokens of friendship and did not know what to do to express his thanks.

It was a day we'll long remember.

U.E.

A HOLIDAY MEAL

It was a Saturday evening. We were eating at my in-laws and one member of the family began attacking me about religion. It was not the first time—but it was worse than before. He not only attacked me, but a lot of other people as well. This hurt me very much. I was unable to resist and I told him off. Then I began to cry, and left without saying goodnight or anything. What made it even worse was that these same people were coming to dinner at my home the following day.

I hardly slept that night and Sunday morning the atmosphere in the house was rather heavy. I did not feel at all like preparing the meal or even going to church. I was heartbroken and tears kept coming back. I went to church just the same, but full of questions—I felt that I had to do something, but it was hard.

In his homily, the parish priest kept speaking about forgiveness, saying that we had to love the people around us, that we had to take the first step... I kept thinking: "Look at that! He knows my problem."

I had been asked to prepare and read one of the general intercessions for the prayer of the faithful. I had written: "The Lord is inviting us today to celebrate in an authentic way. Let us pray that we may be able to respond to this invitation by living the Gospel." Reading it I was forced to decide what I would do. I asked Jesus to help me take this step, and all of a sudden I felt calm, peaceful. I understood I had forgiven. I cannot even describe what I felt: a great interior peace. Afterwards, the holiday meal preparations went very well and all my work ran smoothly. I understood later on that from the moment I accepted the help of Jesus, it was really no longer I who was acting.

C.V.

A RAY OF SUNSHINE

A priest who distributes the Word of Life in a prison says: "Those who live it have changed their attitude toward each other and toward me. Every month we meet together. They listen attentively, even though, for the moment, few share what they live."

And a young prisoner writes: "For me, each month's Word of Life is like a ray of sunshine."

W.C.

12

You truly possess
what you give away

"Sell all your belongings and give the money to the poor. Provide for yourselves purses that don't wear out, and save your riches in heaven, where they will never decrease, because no thief can get to them, no moth can destroy them." (Lk 12:33)

Are you young, aspiring to a life which has an ideal, which is totally committing and calls for a complete change in you? Then listen to Jesus, because no one else in the world will ask as much of you. You are being given an opportunity to prove your faith, your generosity, and your heroism.

Are you an adult, longing for a sound way of life that is committing and yet will not disillusion you? Or are you an older person, wanting to give the last years of your life to someone who will not deceive you, to live without worries that wear you out?

These words of Jesus are also for you.

They conclude a series of admonishments in which Jesus asks you not to worry over what you will eat or what you will wear but, rather, to act as the birds of the air which do not sow, and the lilies of the field which do not weave. Banish, therefore, from your heart all anxieties over the things of this earth. The Father, who loves you more than the birds and the flowers, will take care of you himself.

This is why Jesus tells you, *"Sell all your belongings and give the money to the poor. Provide for yourselves purses that don't wear out, and save your riches in heaven, where they will never decrease, because no thief can get to them, no moth can destroy them."*

In its entirety, and in every word it contains, the Gospel demands everything from you: everything you are and all that you possess.

Prior to Christ's coming into the world, God had never made such radical demands. In the Old Testament, earthly riches were seen as a good, as a blessing from God. Giving alms to the needy was demanded, but as a means to obtain the benevolence of the Almighty. Later on, the idea of a reward in the next life became more commonly accepted among members of the Jewish faith. A king, who had been reprimanded for having squandered his possessions, replied, "My ancestors accumulated treasures for this life, but I have accumulated treasures for the next one." In general, however, Jews did not see any contradiction between accumulating wealth here on earth and preparing a treasure in heaven.

The originality of Jesus' words lies in the fact that he demands a total gift. He asks everything from you. He doesn't want you to be overly concerned about the things of this world. Rather, he wants you to rely on him alone.

He knows that earthly wealth is a tremendous obstacle for you because it can occupy your heart, whereas he wants to possess your heart for himself. This is why he urges you, *"Sell all your belongings and give the money to the poor. Provide for yourselves purses that don't wear out, and save your riches in heaven, where they will never decrease, because no thief can get to them, no moth can destroy them."*

If you cannot physically rid yourself of your possessions, because of family ties or other responsibilities, or if your position in life demands that you live in a certain way, still you should detach yourself from them spiritually, being no more than their administrator. In this way, while dealing with wealth you can love others, and by administering it on their behalf, you can accumulate a treasure which moths cannot destroy, nor thieves carry off.

But are you sure that you should keep all that you possess? Listen to the voice of God within you; and if you cannot decide on your own, seek someone's advice. Then you will discover how many superfluous things there are among your possessions. Do not keep them. Give. Give to those who have not. Put into practice these words of Jesus, "Sell...and give." If you do this, you will fill up purses which do not wear out.

Since you live in the world, it is only logical that you should be concerned with money and other material things. However, God does not want you to be preoccupied with them. So only be concerned with securing that amount which is indispensable for you to live in accordance with your needs. As for the rest, *"Sell all your belongings and give the money to the poor. Provide for yourselves purses that don't wear out, and save your riches in heaven, where they will never decrease, because no thief can get to them, no moth can destroy them."*

Pope Paul VI was truly poor. The way in which he wanted to be buried ("in a plain coffin in the bare earth") proved this. Shortly before dying he told his brother, "My suitcases for that important trip have been ready for some time."

This is what you should do, too: prepare your suitcase.

In the time of Jesus it may have been called "purse," but the meaning is the same. Prepare it day by day. Fill it with things that might be useful to others. You truly possess that which you give away. Think of how much hunger there is in the world, how much suffering, how many needs...

Put every act of love and every deed done for your neighbor into your suitcase as well.

Do everything for God, telling him in your heart, "This is for you." Perform every action well, perfectly, because it is destined for heaven. It will remain for eternity.

Chiara Lubich

Through friends we learned of a very poor woman who had been in the hospital for the past few months.

We went to visit her and found that she needed assitance to eat, but that the hospital was short-staffed, so she was often without help. We described her plight to our friends who live the Word of Life, and we all began to take turns visiting her. The doctors saw that her condition—which was considered hopeless—began to improve and to respond to treatment, and she herself began to smile.

Not long after, the lady in the next bed died. In her will, she left a small sum to help the family of this lady.

C.C.

IT ALL BEGAN WITH A LETTER

It all began in 1968 with a letter from Togo requesting basic medical supplies. A dentist friend began to provide us with medical samples she received, and thus we were able to send a few packages over the course of the next few years.

Some skeptical acquaintances told us: "It's only a drop in the bucket..." They were probably right. However, as we talked about it to other friends, we found many willing to help. A doctor's wife persuaded her husband to give us some of his samples. Several interested nurses and medical students contacted other doctors for us. And many people began giving us the unused medicines left over from treatments they had undergone.

At Christmas 1970 we received a long letter from our friends in Togo recounting many details of life there and saying: "If it weren't for you, we would have nothing.... You are the indispensable instruments of God's providence which enable us to continue our work." We felt, however, that we were doing very little and that we had to do more. Other people joined us. One pharmacist, besides giving us the medical samples he received from sales representatives, persuaded many of his customers to bring their unused drugs back to the pharmacy—for Togo. As a result, year by year the volume of our shipments increased—35 kg in 1971; 108 kg in 1974; 270 kg in 1977.

We also had to think of administrative costs. For example, mailing one three-kilogram package (maximum allowable weight) cost 13.40 francs. To cover the expenses, a group was formed to do such things as embroidery, knitting, and saving baby clothes. These items are sold once a year.

A true climate of friendship has grown up among the participants in this program, and the good will continues to multiply. Some office workers save cartons and wrapping paper destined to be thrown away; other people share in the work of sorting, which they do at home. Each person does what he or she has to do. The routine could desensitize us, but the letters we get from Togo protect us from this possible danger.

Besides the general news, each letter gives us particular details about how the contents of the parcels have been used. Often, a certain medicine has arrived just at the time when it was needed. This information gives us the assurance that we are really helping to save human lives.

"...This afternoon a mother and three children arrived. She had a fever of 105° F. The examination showed typhoid. Your parcels arrived and contained precisely the medicine we needed."

Or again: "We were able to continue regulating a patient's blood pressure without interruption because the medicine arrived exactly on the day we needed it."

This year we will pass the 300 kg mark, which is close to the limit of what our group can do. But many similar projects are now going on elsewhere. Starting is the hardest part; but it is amazing to discover how many people are just looking for such an opportunity to help.

M.B.
(France)

A PAY RAISE

I am 20 years old and I work as a laborer in a shipyard. For some time now I have been living the Word of Life and consequently I do my work well. The foreman told me he had noticed my improved performance and had decided to give me a raise. Later, thinking of the Word of Life: "Sell all your belongings..." I suddenly remembered another laborer, the father of a large family who is burdened by a lot of problems. He needed a raise much more than I. So I went to see my boss and suggested that he give the raise to this fellow worker. The foreman was utterly astonished, but he agreed.

P.L.

13
Love to the very end

"He had loved his own in this world, and would show his love for them to the end." (Jn 13:1)

Do you know where this sentence appears in the Gospel? It is found in St. John's account of the last supper when Jesus is about to wash the feet of his disciples and is preparing for his passion.

During the last moments that Jesus spent with his own, he revealed in the highest and most explicit way the love he had always had for them.

"He had loved his own in this world, and would show his love for them to the end." The words *"to the end"* mean to the end of his life, to his very last breath. But there is also the idea of perfection, that is to say, he loved them completely, totally, with extreme intensity, to the highest degree.

The disciples would stay in the world while Jesus would go to his glory. They would feel alone, they would have many trials to face. It is precisely in view of those moments that Jesus wanted to make them feel sure of his love.

"He had loved his own in this world, and would show his love for them to the end." Don't you see reflected in this sentence Jesus' style of life and way of loving? He even washed the feet of his disciples. His love made him stoop to do this lowly service which in those days was done only by slaves.

After having given them his extraordinary words, his miracles and all the other things he had done, Jesus was now preparing for the tragedy of Calvary in which he would give his very life for *"his own"* and for all people. He knew they had a great need, the greatest need any human being can have: the need to be liberated from sin, which means freed from death, and to regain the possibility of entering the kingdom of heaven. Only he could give them the peace and joy of everlasting life.

And so he gave himself totally, to the point that, before he died, he even felt forsaken by the Father. Having thus loved to the end, he was able to say, "It is accomplished."

"He had loved his own in this world, and would show his love for them to the end." We see in these words both the tenacity of God's love and the tender affection of a brother. Since Christ lives in us, we Christians can also love like this.

But it is not the imitation of Jesus in actually dying for others (when his hour came) that I propose to you right now. Nor do I hold up to you models like Father Kolbe who died for a fellow prisoner, or Father Damien who contracted leprosy with the lepers and died with them and for them.

It may be that in the course of your lifetime you will never be asked to give your physical life for your neighbor. But what God certainly does ask of you is that you love them "to the end," to the point where you too can say, "It is accomplished."

This is what eleven-year-old Lisa, who lives in Italy, has done. She saw that her classmate and friend Giorgina was extremely sad. She tried to comfort her, but to no avail. So she decided to find out why her friend was so sad. She learned that Giorgina's father had died and that her mother had left her alone with her grandmother, and had gone to live with another man. Now aware of the tragedy, Lisa decided to do something about it. Though she was only a little girl, she asked Giorgina to let her talk to her mother, but Giorgina begged her to first go with her to visit her father's grave. With great love Lisa went with her and overheard her sobbing and imploring her father to take her with him. Lisa felt heart-broken. There was a little old church in the cemetery and the two girls went in. The only things left inside the church were a small tabernacle and a crucifix. Lisa said, "Look, everything in this world is going to be destroyed; but the crucifix and the Eucharist will always be with us." Giorgina dried her tears and replied, "Yes, you are right!" Then with tender love Lisa took Giorgina by the hand and accompanied her to her mother. When they got there Lisa turned to the mother and said, "I know this is none of my business, but I am telling you that you left your daughter without a mother's love which she needs so badly, and I'm telling you also that you will never have peace until you repent and take your child back to live with you."

The following day Lisa met Giorgina in school and lovingly tried to cheer her up. But something new happened that day: a car came to pick Giorgina up after school. It was her mother. From that day on, the car has kept coming regularly because Giorgina now lives with her mother who no longer has any relationship with the man she was living with.

Looking at the small, but significant, thing Lisa did, we can now say, "It is accomplished." She did everything well "to the end," and she achieved what she set out to do.

Think about it. How many times have you started to take an interest in someone who needed help and then abandoned him or her, using all kinds of excuses to silence your conscience? How many things have you started with enthusiasm and then stopped because of difficulties you felt were beyond your strength?

This is the lesson Jesus is giving you today: *"He had loved his own in this world, and would show his love for them to the end."*

Love to the very end—and if one day God should actually ask you for your life, then, like the martyrs who went to their death singing, you will not hesitate. And your reward shall be the greatest glory because Jesus said that no one has greater love than the one who gives his life for his friends.

Chiara Lubich

Some time ago our neighbor's husband died, leaving her with two young daughters and an older son. Since then we have tried to let her feel our friendship by sharing little gifts from time to time, such as a bunch of flowers or cakes for the children. When Christmas arrived, we invited them to our home so that the father's absence would not be so painful. It was a simple evening. We played with the little girls, and everyone contributed to create a happy atmosphere. After a while it seemed that heaven was not so far away; and together we talked of heaven and their father.

Then other problems came along. First, the son had a serious accident. We immediately went to the hospital to visit him, and assured him that we would look after the family, of which he was now the sole support. He became calm then, and stopped worrying. This was our contribution to his recovery.

Then it was the grandmother: the doctors had discovered an inoperable cancer. She remained with the family, but our efforts to get assistance for home care were unsuccessful. Her treatments were long and difficult, but one of us, being a nurse, was able to show the family how to administer them. In time, even the doctor stopped coming since there was nothing more he could do. This was a heavy burden, but we carried it together and our relationship deepened.

The moment came when we could start to speak to the grandmother of how to live, as well as possible, each moment given to her. We knew that in this way, she would be preparing herself for heaven. We notified the parish priest who began to bring her communion regularly. Little by little the grandmother realized that we were living in unity with her and she asked us to pray with her. To express her gratitude she had her daughter buy a few small gifts for us.

During this time our neighbor's faith was strengthened because we had shared these trials with her. One day she spoke about this openly, adding: "Even though I continue believing and loving, I sometimes ask myself, 'Why? Why all this?'"

Together we recalled the moment when Jesus felt abandoned by his Father and cried out: "My God, my God, why have you forsaken me?" Then peace returned to her. That same day she confided in us how she missed her husband's presence and his help. We prayed together, entrusting her husband to the communion of saints. Comforted, she was once more able to speak of him to the children.

In a few weeks the two daughters will be confirmed, and one of us was asked to be godmother with these words: "I entrust her to you; I am certain that she is in good hands. And in this way we will all be part of the same family." All this seems to us the hundredfold of the Gospel we have been trying to live. It shows us that God was at work.

In fact, we have discovered that our way of life holds a certain fascination for our neighbors and also for people in our parish. A neighbor told us just the other day: "I, too, want to do something for you, because you do things for Jesus." And to celebrate her decision she brought over some crepes she had made for us.

L.F.

THE UNSEEN GIFT

A worker in the group I supervise was about to turn 65, and would soon have to retire. Some time before, my boss had told him he could remain until the end of the year. However, the man was often absent, and what work he did was done poorly. He had been warned about this several times, but to no avail. Consequently, at the beginning of last month, my boss reconsidered his decision and told the man, in front of me, that he would have to leave the company at the end of the month.

The next day, when I greeted him as usual, I was completely rebuffed. I realized that there was now a wall between us. I tried to start a conversation, but he immediately began bombarding me with grievances. The peace that had previously existed between us was gone, and I felt it had to be re-established. But all his accusations had sowed doubts in me: Perhaps I *had* made gross errors in his regard. Perhaps my attitude *had* been hyprocritical. I could not see the matter clearly. Then the Word of Life came to my rescue, helping me to keep going and to keep loving. I understood that most of this person's aggressiveness stemmed from the fact that I had not been able to understand and defend his behavior.

I wondered how I could go about re-establishing peace. In the meantime I noticed that my relationship with the others was deteriorating. It was not an easy time and I often felt very lonely. But in this situation I discovered that Jesus loves me a great deal.

I felt that it was important that this retirement be celebrated, while I remained in the background. It was then that the administration asked me to organize a collection for his departure. I also planned to chip in with the others for a gift— but they took up the collection one morning when I was out, and coldly told me what they thought of me when I later asked if I could chip in. So, after discussing it with my wife, I gave him a personal gift, unknown to the rest of them. On the day he left, I was happy to discover that this gesture had re-established good relations between us.

My other colleagues know nothing of this gift. At work things continue to be difficult and tense, and a heavy atmosphere seems to reign. The other evening, as I came home worn out and on the verge of tears, I had the impression I was experiencing my Gethsemane. I do not know what the days ahead have in store for me. But I am at peace.

J.B.